Grenville C. Gilbert

23rd August, 2021.

PARABLES OF TIME AND ETERNITY

Parables of TIME *and* ETERNITY

Keith Ward

CASCADE *Books* • Eugene, Oregon

PARABLES OF TIME AND ETERNITY

Cascade Books
An Imprint of Wipf and Stock Publishers
199 W. 8th Ave., Suite 3
Eugene, OR 97401

www.wipfandstock.com

PAPERBACK ISBN: 978-1-7252-8843-0
HARDCOVER ISBN: 978-1-7252-8844-7
EBOOK ISBN: 978-1-7252-8845-4

Cataloguing-in-Publication data:

Names: Ward, Keith, author.

Title: Parables of time and eternity / Keith Ward.

Description: Eugene, OR: Cascade Books, 2021 | Includes bibliographical references.

Identifiers: ISBN 978-1-7252-8843-0 (paperback) | ISBN 978-1-7252-8844-7 (hardcover) | ISBN 978-1-7252-8845-4 (ebook)

Subjects: LCSH: Jesus Christ—Parables | Parables | Kingdom of God | Bible—Theology

Classification: BT375.3 W37 2021 (print) | BT375.3 (ebook)

Contents

Acknowledgements

I GRATEFULLY ACKNOWLEDGE THE help and advice of Robert Morgan, of Oxford University, and Robin Parry, my editor. They should not, however, be held responsible for the views I express.

PART ONE

Why the Parables of Jesus Are Important

HOW PHILOSOPHY MAY APPEAL TO REVELATION

When I wrote *Sharing in the Divine Nature*[1] I thought of it as the completion of my attempt to expound the Christian faith in terms of a form of personal idealism. In its Christian form, this is the belief that God is a personal being of the greatest possible value, who realizes the divine nature as love by creating free and developing communities of persons, with the ultimate goal of uniting them in the closest way to the divine self.

One major thing remained unclear, however. Why should these beliefs essentially depend upon Jesus? Might the figure of Jesus not just be a constructed ideal of the unity of divine and human, who might never have existed in history? The biblical story of Jesus might be a parable, a fictional account of what an ideal human being, if fully conscious of the presence of God and filled with the power of God, would be like. The parable could be based, in some cloudy way, on a real historical figure, but that figure could be a provincial faith-healer, exorcist, and peripatetic preacher, whose life had later been fantasized well beyond historical reality.

One modern New Testament scholar, John Dominic Crossan, suggests something very like this.[2] He accepts that a historical Jesus probably existed, but the Gospel accounts of his life largely consist of fictional ideals, imagined speeches, and the occurrence of impossible miracles. Nevertheless, he holds it probable that Jesus was a preacher of non-violent justice

1. Eugene, OR: Cascade, 2020.
2. Crossan, *Power of Parable*.

and love, and that the existence of such a person is important, because it shows that a life empowered by God is possible. He says this proves that "at least one human being could cooperate fully with God,"[3] and that this can serve as an inspiration to us.

However, on purely historical grounds it does not seem at all probable that we could be sure that an individual human being—whether Jesus or someone else—cooperated fully with God, or that only one such person in human history ever did so. Such a claim seems far beyond the bounds of historical verification, even if it concerned a person alive today let alone someone who died thousands of years ago. How could we possibly know this? That might be part of the fiction too, in which case it does not show that such a life is possible at all.

It also seems that personal idealism can exist without Jesus. It may seem that it is a general philosophy, not as such committed to any particular and specific historical claims. Yet, on reflection, it appears that it must make some historical claims, some claims about what happens in the universe. For a start, it claims that there is a spiritual and personal being on whom the whole universe depends. It claims that the nature of this being is love—and if that is not to be vacuous, it entails that there must be some historical events that manifest the love of God. There must, it seems, be some particular events in which the love of God is experienced and has some effect on what happens. It also claims that God has a purpose, so there must be a future in which the union of divinity and humanity is realized. And there must be some reason to think there is such a purpose.

If there is such a God, it is highly probable that God will cause some events in history that manifest the divine nature as love and give some idea of the divine purpose. Such events might not be so spectacular that no one could ignore them, but they must be strong enough to give evidence that God is indeed loving and purposeful. Personal idealism therefore increases the probability that there will be events of revelation in history, events disclosing the nature and purpose of God. If that is so, it follows that some historical claims will be relevant to philosophical claims, even if it is difficult to pin down exactly what they are.

It is sometimes objected that claims about history can only be made with probability, and so cannot give rise to certainty, whereas philosophical claims should not depend on contingent and contested claims about history. That, however, is not the case. Virtually all philosophical claims

3. Crossan, *Power of Parable*, 256.

are contested and differ considerably depending on the philosophers who make them. The philosopher Lessing famously complained about "the ugly broad ditch" between accidental truths of history and necessary truths of reason.[4] But the philosophy of personal idealism—or any competing philosophy, such as scientific naturalism or materialism—is by no means a necessary truth of reason. It is a hypothesis, based on a confluence of many factors that seems to converge on it. All philosophical hypotheses are highly disputed, so we cannot avoid probability. Probability just has to be sufficient for total commitment, if the cause is good and if a great deal is at stake, because nothing more than probability is available to us. That is true both in philosophy and in faith, except that in faith more is at stake, since a whole practical way of life, perhaps a life of self-sacrifice, is in question.

So we must ask what makes it probable to some of us that there is a God, that the divine nature is love, and that we are destined for union with God. The answer will lie in some historical facts, and in some human experiences, either of public events or in subjective experiences, whether ours or the experience of others. Those facts are likely to include claims to have experienced some form of revelation from something like God.

JESUS AS PART OF A DEVELOPING REVELATORY TRADITION

When we examine such facts, we must be aware that we do not start with a blank slate. We have all learned from others about many things. And we have learned things about God from others. Since we are not omniscient and are of very limited experience, we will do well to cast our net widely, and listen to the testimony of many people who seem to be intelligent, experienced, and competent in the things we wish to know about. At that point, if not before, we should become aware that we have not just conjured up ideas of God, love, and the consummation of all things out of our own minds and experiences. There is a history of developing, and often contrasting, ideas of God or of spiritual reality.

The idea of a God of love originated in the Jewish tradition of faith, and a line of developing thought about what this means can be traced in the Hebrew scriptures. The idea of an ultimate union with God is a relatively

4. Lessing, "On the Proof of the Spirit and of Power," 55.

late development in that tradition, but the seeds of it are there, for instance in the prophetic image of a "marriage" of God and Israel.[5]

That tradition seems to find a specifically non-vindictive and non-violent form in many parts of the recorded teachings of Jesus. Dominic Crossan is right about that. He is also right to point out that the New Testament still contains some vindictive and judgmental and violent elements. 2 Thessalonians 1:8, for instance, is one of the worst, when Jesus is predicted to return "in flaming fire, inflicting vengeance on those who do not know God." Twist and turn as one will, it is hard not to see this as manifesting a desire for violent revenge on one's enemies—a thing that the Jesus of the Sermon on the Mount roundly condemns.

There are two main points here. One is that the idea of a non-violent, loving God, who is concerned with the whole world and with a good purpose that will be realized in a world to come, did find clear expression in parts of the New Testament. The other is that there are other parts of the New Testament that have not escaped from a rather violent, vengeful attitude that seems to rejoice in the destruction of its enemies. The New Testament is not all peace and joy; but it does speak of peace and joy as the marks of a mature and morally acceptable faith. This, I agree with Crossan, argues for the records of Jesus' teaching being basically reliable, especially when they run counter to many of the expectations of a liberated kingdom of Israel that some disciples were hoping for.

While it is impossible to find proof on purely historical grounds that Jesus "cooperated fully with God," there is evidence in the Gospels that Jesus taught non-violent care for the outcasts of society, and stressed that God was a forgiving, merciful lover of all creation, especially of those who had at one time rejected love, and were not conventionally good or pious. Jesus apparently felt a close relationship with God, whom he called *abba*, father. He is recorded as adopting a view of himself as one anointed by God (the "Messiah") to bring the Jewish tradition of faith to a new and climactic point of change. And if it is true that he appeared to his disciples after his physical death, this suggests a unique role in the disclosure of the divine nature and purpose. It would show, for instance, that there is life in the world to come, and that Jesus discloses this in a remarkable and definitive way. This is enough to make an assertion of some form of divine-human unity in his person a living possibility.

5. Isaiah 62:4.

The idea of God is not just spun out of a philosopher's head. The idea has a developing history, and philosophies have a developing history also. In the Jewish tradition, the idea of God has mainly originated in the experiences of prophetic figures, in events of revelation, when God was believed to "speak" to the prophets, or to disclose things about the divine contract of union with Israel. Philosophy does not come first; it springs from reflection on experience. Personal idealism, though it has its roots in Plato and Aristotle, has developed through Aquinas, Leibniz, Kant, Hegel, and others. It includes reflection on the claimed experiences of revelation in the Jewish and later in the Christian faith, on the sense of personal presence, the sense of moral demand, and the sense of providential guidance and purpose that has always been part of that faith. Philosophy has not preceded this sense; rather, much philosophy has built upon it.

Jesus has played an important part in this process, before anyone invented personal idealism. He is recorded as claiming an intimate awareness of divine presence, as preaching that this presence was both morally demanding and endlessly forgiving, as promising that humans would attain their fulfilment in the world to come, and, most importantly, as appearing after his death, if the disciples are to be believed. These claims are possible data for philosophy, not conclusions of philosophy. They give the person of Jesus, as it is recorded by some of his disciples, a revelatory status—he is a historical point at which something new and crucial about spiritual reality is unveiled.

This revelatory status implies that Jesus was in a uniquely favorable position to know God's presence, demand, and promise. Within the New Testament itself, most explicitly in the Gospel of John, this was construed as a unique union of divine and human in the person of Jesus ("the Word became flesh").[6] It is not surprising that in my own formulations of personal idealism, I have in fact relied very largely not just on the writings of past philosophers (who were themselves influenced by Jewish or Christian faith) but on the biblical testimonies to a decisive revelation of God in Jesus. For this is what gives assertions about a God of love with a good purpose for all creation a grounding in real history. It is not just imaginative speculation. It is based on a reflective working out of the implications of Jesus' life and teachings for our understanding of our place in the universe.

6. John 1:14.

JESUS' PARABLES AND THE GOSPEL OF JOHN

In this way some philosophical affirmations do depend on some assertions about Jesus, and that might include accepting the truth of his main recorded teachings. But there is still a problem. My view, for instance, is explicitly based on John's Gospel and on some, but not all, New Testament documents. The problem is this: almost all biblical scholars agree that the first three Gospels, the so-called "Synoptic" Gospels, do not contain any explicit teachings by Jesus about his own status as the Light of the World or the Bread of Life, or about the union of God, Jesus, and humanity. Yet the Synoptic Gospels, by wide agreement, most likely represent what Jesus actually taught—and this is expressed most vividly in short and often cryptic parables, none of which occur in John's Gospel.

Because this is so, some scholars, like Adolf von Harnack, have said that Jesus' original gospel message was simply about the fatherhood of God, the infinite value of the human soul, the command of love, and the transforming presence of God in the hearts of men and women.[7] It was not, claimed Harnack, about Jesus' own status, his unique union with God, or about some mystical union between God and humanity or God and Jesus. Perhaps, on this account, the Johannine vision of such a union, perfectly manifest in Jesus, is a later invention of the early church, which had begun to forget the simplicity of the original message of Jesus.

In this book I want to address this problem. If Harnack's view is correct, then the revelatory source of much Christian faith is not Jesus, but some unknown group's quasi-gnostic theories (John, on this view, was a quasi-gnostic) projected back onto Jesus.

The obvious trouble with views like that of Harnack is that John (whoever he was) and the churches of which he was part almost certainly believed that what they were saying was true. They did not see themselves as pinning some new theory of divine-human unity onto the extant memories about Jesus. By reflecting on the memories about Jesus and the impact he had on his disciples they came to think that he was more than a prophet, that he was in some sense uniquely united to God.

Jesus had not just taught some new facts about God. He had declared that the kingdom, the rule, of God had come, and he had convinced his disciples that in this kingdom he was the King, anointed as such by God. Even in the Synoptic Gospels, which rarely, if ever, make explicit divine

7. Harnack, *What is Christianity?* Lecture 1.

claims for Jesus, their master spoke with the authority of God. It was a Johannine *insight*, not a Johannine invention, that this reality called for a unique union of divine and human in Jesus, and John's Gospel begins to work out the implications of this. Jesus remains the ultimate authority, and John's Gospel begins to explore what that means for Jesus' role and status in human history.

If the Johannine view is a working out of the implications of the Synoptic records about Jesus, then the parables of the Synoptic Gospels can be interpreted in an expansive way so as to make John's view of Jesus, as a cosmic spiritual reality embodied in a human form, already present to those who have ears to hear it in the parables.

I shall suggest that the parables of Jesus can be interpreted in such an expansive way. Indeed, I shall suggest that they can be interpreted in an even more expansive way to give support to a form of personal idealism—though I do not mean to suggest that my view is the only possible one.

I do not intend to provide a detailed historical or linguistic analysis of or commentary on the parables. This has been done very effectively by Jülicher, Dodd, Jeremias, Crossan, and Scott, among many others. I shall presuppose their work in what I say, and I am not going to dispute the points they make about the cultural and linguistic forms and contexts of the parables. I shall, however, have comments to make about what they take to be the original meaning or structure of the parables. This is for two main reasons. First, I argue John's Gospel gives a correct spelling out of who Jesus was and what he taught, and many modern accounts do not make this clear; indeed, many even reject the idea that John correctly represents Jesus. Second, I aim to give an expansive interpretation of some main parables, suggesting that they express a universally relevant teaching that can be naturally developed into a form of personal idealism. In the modern age a number of relatively new factors have changed the way ancient religious traditions must be seen. Among them are a global view of the history of religions, an acceptance of modern science, especially evolutionary theory, a post-Enlightenment stress on the autonomy of the human will, and a central concern that religion should aim at the welfare of all sentient beings.[8] Jesus' recorded parables need to be interpreted in a way that takes full account of these factors. If this can be done, it will be seen that Jesus was a teacher of wisdom that is as relevant for us as it was for the Galilean disciples who first heard him speak. In those apparently simple stories, the

8. These factors are spelled out more fully in Ward, *Religion in the Modern World*.

nature and purpose of God for *all* creation was expressed. My aim is to show that this is so.

SEEKING THE HISTORICAL JESUS

The historical Jesus is not recoverable by the use of purely historical methods. There have been many searches for the historical Jesus, and their most marked characteristic is that most of them have come to different conclusions. At one extreme, it has been said that "Jesus" is a fictional construction from Old Testament texts mixed with some ancient Egyptian and Greek mythical figures. At the other extreme, there have been people who have tried to "harmonize" the four Gospels into one literal, true, and exact record of a man who lived in Galilee. In between those extremes, there are scholars who have thought Jesus was a prophet of a catastrophic divine intervention in human history that would eliminate evil and bring about an age of perfect peace and justice. Some have seen Jesus as a Zealot, a social revolutionary against the power of Rome, who ultimately failed in his mission. He has been seen as the founder of one true holy and ultimately Roman Church, and as a radical teacher who was opposed to all institutional and hierarchical religious groups.

The vast majority of scholars who have carefully examined the four Gospels have agreed that Jesus did exist, that he had a reputation as a healer and exorcist, that he gathered disciples, that he criticized the religious leaders of his day, that he was crucified, and that he was charismatic enough to be taken as the Messiah, or anointed one, who was thought by many to be delivering Israel from domination, in some sense. Beyond that, there is little that historians who use modern analytical and critical methods agree on. That is what I mean by saying that the historical Jesus is not recoverable by purely historical methods.

What other methods are there to investigate a historical figure? There are a number of factors that lead scholars to assign different probabilities to the evidence before them. This is true of all historical matters, especially those fairly remote in history. For instance, someone who holds that all events are governed by general laws, and that humans are pretty gullible, is unlikely to give a high probability to accounts of miraculous healings. Someone who does not believe in demons is likely to discount reports of the exorcisms of such demons, especially when they speak and complain, as they do in the Gospels. Someone who holds that the world is purely material is very unlikely to believe in reports of resurrection. General beliefs like these, about what things are in general likely to happen, will lead to discounting many Gospel reports about Jesus.

If you believe in God, or at least are open to the possibility of there being a higher spiritual reality that can have some effects on this physical world, then you are more likely to accept that Jesus could have had exceptional knowledge of this reality and could have been a reliable teacher about its nature. If, in addition, you tend to think that the developing views about God recorded in the Hebrew Bible are on the whole reliable insights into the nature of spiritual reality—that there is in fact a personal God who makes moral demands on humans and has a good purpose for them—you will be more open to the possibility that Jesus stood in the Jewish prophetic tradition, and that he in some way fulfilled that tradition, as the Gospels say he did. Perhaps he clarified and intensified those demands, and showed more clearly what the purpose was, or even inaugurated a new stage in the realization of that purpose.

While it is impossible to achieve a neutral and historically verifiable account of what Jesus said, much less of how he saw his own person and calling, we can and should place Jesus in his historical context, the context of Galilean Judaism. We can assume that he was brought up with the beliefs and practices of such a society. So we can be fairly sure that he believed in the God of Abraham and Isaac, in a covenant of unity and faithfulness between God and the people of Israel, in the teachings of the prophets, and that he was familiar with the expectation of a messianic figure, however vaguely conceived, who would realize the true vocation and destiny of Israel in world history.

Standing within this tradition, could he have seen himself as the Gospels present him, as the "King of the Jews," a Davidic monarch anointed by God to bring the history of Israel to a dramatic point of fulfilment? I think it is clear that he could have, since he was not alone among the Jews of his day in making that sort of claim. Other claimants to be "saviours of Israel" are known to have existed at around that time, and the Gospels record that he needed to warn against "false messiahs." He could even have seen himself as an embodiment of Torah, or of divine Wisdom, since that also is a claim that has been made on behalf of some eminent Rabbis.[9] It is quite thinkable,

9. In the Talmud of the Land of Israel or Yerushalmi, c. 400 CE, the Torah came to be represented in the person of the sage, who was, in himself, the Torah incarnate. See Neusner, "Is the God of Judaism Incarnate?" 214.

and it actually happened, that some Rabbis could be seen as so learned in the Torah, and so completely living out its precepts, that they could be seen as human embodiments of the Torah, of eternal divine Wisdom. This would, of course, never have been put by saying that these Rabbis "were God," or were divine. But it could plausibly be put by saying that they were "sons of God," as the Davidic kings were called in the Psalms (Ps 2:7). And if that was the case with Jesus, he could well have seen himself as having the vocation of passing on that Wisdom to his disciples, and through them to a wider community. Jesus would be a teacher of Wisdom, and even perhaps a human embodiment of divine Wisdom. Such things are not outside the bounds of even quite an orthodox form of Judaism.

This is how Jesus is presented in some New Testament documents, especially in the Gospel of John, for whom Jesus is "the Word [the *Logos* or Wisdom of God] made flesh," and in letters like those to the Colossians and Ephesians, which present Christ as the one in and through whom the universe was created, and as the one in whom all things in the universe ("in heaven and earth") will be united. More exactly, Jesus was a man in and through whom that cosmic figure of Christ, the eternal Word, the pattern and goal of creation, was embodied.

These things are real possibilities for such a person as Jesus. His life and teachings could have given rise to such claims about him, and he could even have made them, in some perhaps cryptic form, about himself. If we ask whether such claims could have been justified, we need to resort to a set of background beliefs about whether there is a God, whether God has made a covenant of union with Israel, and whether any of the prophets were genuine. I do not suppose there will be agreement on these questions. In that sense, there is no possible access to the historical Jesus. But we can at least say that these sorts of claims about him are not incredible, and could, given the truth of various other background beliefs, have been justifiably made.

JESUS AS A SPIRIT PERSON

What would have justified the belief that Jesus was Messiah, Son of God, and a King in the house of David? I am not here trying to probe the secrets of the mind of Jesus. That is totally impossible, historically speaking. I am asking what might justify a person's belief that they were an embodiment of divine Wisdom, bringing the rule of God into the world in a new way.

First of all, we need to admit that, in many different areas of human activity, there are some exceptional individuals who seem almost superhuman in their abilities. We have probably all heard of mathematical geniuses who can solve mathematical problems that most people could not even understand. In music, composers like Bach and Mozart did things that most professional musicians could never hope to do. In soccer, some players have abilities that seem to be beyond ordinary human competence.

The point is that we might expect that, in respect of knowledge of the presence and purpose of God, there will be some outstanding individuals who have a more intense sense of the divine presence and purpose for their lives than is even conceivable for the rest of us. In many religions, there are people who have claimed a sense of union with the Divine. We might call them the "mystics" of spiritual life. Marcus Borg helpfully calls them "Spirit persons."[10] There are people who experience a divine calling to devote their lives to a specific goal, leaving aside almost everything else. Some, of course, are deluded. But if there is a God with a purpose, we might expect that some will be genuine. They will be spiritual teachers, in some sense one with God, who can teach us how to live a fuller spiritual life.

If we look carefully at the religions of the world, we will find that there are many such teachers, or claimants to be such teachers. They live in very different religious traditions. They would include Sankara in the Indian tradition of Vedanta, Gautama Buddha in a non-theistic path that nonetheless spoke of a spiritual journey and goal, Lao-Tzu, who was claimed to have insight into the "Way of Heaven," the wisdom of living a fulfilled life in harmony with the ultimate nature of things, Guru Nanak, the founder of Sikhism, and many others. Jesus could be seen as such a one.

You might say, correctly, they cannot all be right. They each lived within a specific tradition of beliefs and values, in such a way that they could be said both to fulfil and to transform that tradition in new ways. Jesus would fit into this pattern, as one brought up in priestly Judaism, centred on the Jerusalem Temple, who fulfilled and transformed his tradition by teaching that the prophetically promised way of the Spirit had drawn near in his person.

These different religious traditions cannot all be equally correct. You cannot, for instance, both believe in reincarnation and in the resurrection of the body; you cannot both believe that there is a personal God and that there is no such thing as a substantial continuing self. Yet within many

10. Borg, *Meeting Jesus Again for the First Time.*

traditions (I do not say all) there is a shared concern that there is a way of self-centred attachment that leads to death, and a way of altruistic concern for the welfare of all that leads to life. There is a shared advocacy of moral and spiritual practices that lead to wisdom and compassion. And there is a shared belief that true human fulfilment is to be found in harmony or union with the nature of a reality that is not simply physical, and that has objective value and therefore, in some sense, purpose.

If we are attentive to the range of religious traditions in the world, we can find at least four main ways of filling out these shared beliefs.

1. There is what we might call *a unitive or "mystical" way*, wherein we aim to unite the individual self with the Self of all. This characterizes a range of Indian spiritual paths, notably the tradition called Vedanta, in which Sankara and Ramanuja are outstanding examples.

2. There is *a path of renunciation*, whereby we seek freedom from attachment to the desires of the world. Various forms of Buddhism follow such a path.

3. There is *a way of wisdom*, by which we seek to live in harmony with a fundamentally spiritual dimension of existence. Chinese spiritual traditions often follow this way.

4. And there is *the "prophetic" path*, a way of devotion and personal relationship to the supremely personal deity. This is the path of the God of the spiritual descendants of Abraham and Isaac.

Jesus, as a Jew, belongs primarily to the prophetic path. I suppose that most religious believers would belong to one of these paths, and they would naturally see the other world faiths from the perspective afforded by their own location. But the paths do not have to be completely exclusive. Each tradition can be expansive, being faithful to one basic understanding of spiritual reality, yet extending its understanding by responding to the insights of other traditions as well as to new factual knowledge and moral insights that are gradually attained through time. The prophetic path, the path of which Jesus was part, can expand to embrace aspects of the unitive, renunciatory, and wisdom paths. It is possible for an extraordinarily perceptive Jew to experience a strong sense of union with the Supremely Real, to practice renunciation of wealth and settled home, and to embrace a wisdom that brings insight into the true nature of spiritual life.

If anyone realized these possibilities in the fullest way, such a person could well come to have a virtually unique sense of unity with the Self of all—with God; a unique sense of vocation, being guided to transform in a new way the tradition within which they live; and a unique ability to mediate the healing and reconciling powers of God to those around them. Their experience, their freedom from hatred, greed, and pride, and the powers of insight and healing that they possessed would justify their belief that they had a uniquely intense awareness of God and a unique vocation to both fulfil and transform their inherited tradition.

Jesus, according to the Gospel witness, was such a person. While it is impossible to construct a neutral and verifiable history of what Jesus actually said and did, it is possible to show that Jesus could have believed, and could have been personally justified in believing, that he was called to proclaim a new perspective on the "kingdom of heaven" (the rule of God) that would both fulfil and transform the Judaism of his day. That new perspective is that the rule of God is to come not just in Israel but to *the whole world;* not just in temple ritual, but in an inner vitality of the Spirit; and not just with judgment and condemnation, but with the hope of fulfilment, freedom, and life for all, even for those who are presently enslaved by their own pride, hatred, and greed.

JESUS AS THE EMBODIMENT OF DIVINE WISDOM

It seems to me plausible that John's Gospel was written as a projection of the risen and glorified Jesus—who was claimed to be experienced in the church community—back onto the historical figure of Jesus. Christ, it was believed, really was the Way, the Truth, and the Life, was one with God, and the ultimate goal of creation was to be "in" him. The glorified Jesus manifested the Christ in an open and explicit way, and was experienced by early Christians in this way. Yet during his earthly life these things had been hidden. They were true, but they were not openly disclosed. They were secrets, discernible only to an inner core of disciples, and even then, not fully understood. These secret doctrines were hidden in the form of parables, stories of everyday events in an agricultural culture, but with many strange features and exaggerated details.

The long speeches by Jesus in John are constructions out of memories of Jesus supplemented by experiences of the risen Jesus and by prayerful reflection on the meaning of his life, death, and resurrection. The parables of Jesus are memories of things he taught during his life, teachings that had a clear and direct impact on his hearers, usually in criticism, warning, exhortation, and promise. But they also had a meaning hidden from many, which John's Gospel was to explicate.

Is this truly what the parables teach? I think that it is. On this view, Jesus was not, as some people have thought, a prophet of the end of the world, teaching that history was soon to end with terrible violence, and that a small elect might be saved by the pure mercy of God, if they believed in Jesus' message before it was too late. That is really a very gloomy view, for most of the world, and its God seems to be a rather capricious and impatient tyrant.

Jesus' ministry, it is true, might seem rather restricted, since it lasted for only about three years, and was only directed to "the lost sheep of the house of Israel." Perhaps he had not given up the hope that a reformed Israel could still exercise a priestly ministry to the whole world. But it is reported that he also foresaw the destruction of the temple and maybe of the nation of Israel as a political entity. If the Israel was scattered throughout the world, perhaps the new covenant community of the Spirit would pass on the gospel of the rule of God for all the earth.

It seems to me probable that Jesus, in speaking about the promise of the kingdom, would have used the symbolic language of the prophets about a final fulfilment of God's rule in a perfected earth. But it seems to me inconceivable that he definitely thought the whole created universe would end quite soon, as some interpretations of Jesus as an apocalyptic prophet suggest. The whole tenor of his teaching is that the completed rule of God is not a nationalistic political ascendancy of Israel. Such a thing would only continue the violence (Israel would take revenge on her enemies) and pride (Israel would become top nation) of the world that was to pass away. And if the world ended soon, millions of souls would not be born to inherit the joys of the kingdom.

The prophets used a hugely exaggerated symbolism, which deployed the language of temporal nearness ("quickly") to convey both a sense of the spiritual nearness ("close") and yet also the present incompleteness of God's rule. Jesus used that symbolism too. God's rule is close to us. It is actual in the spiritual world, which is even now at the edge of and breaking into our physical world. So we are wise to act as if it will come quickly, yet also to endure with patience and resolution the tasks that are set before us.

If this is so, then it is entirely reasonable to accept that Jesus could have seen himself as a spiritual reformer and transformer of Jewish tradition. As a spiritual leader with a strong sense of union with God, he was called to bring into the world a new spiritual community that would teach and aim at the union of all created things with supreme Spirit, with God. Such a reformer and critic of the political and spiritual establishment could have foreseen his death, as the Gospels say he did. It would not take much insight to see that his criticisms of the establishment would lead to something unpleasant. Even Plato, four hundred years earlier, had remarked that any truly just man would be "impaled."[11] It might seem more difficult to believe that Jesus could have foreseen his own resurrection, as the Gospels say he did. But Jesus believed in a God who could raise the dead, he is reported as believing that the patriarchs and prophets are alive "in heaven," and as promising that the penitent thief would be "in Paradise" with him on the day of his death. If so, he did believe in life after death, in some sort of bodily form. And he was committed to believing that God would vindicate his ministry in some way after his death.

It is not necessary to suppose that Jesus had a clear idea of exactly what this vindication would consist in. If he was truly human, he would not have had a clear and inerrant vision of the future. The biblical prophets did not have such clarity, as is apparent from the fact that their prophecies were in some important respects rarely literally fulfilled—Israel never triumphed politically over all her enemies, as the prophets had often said they would. Nevertheless, the prophets had a strong sense of divine judgment on injustice, and on the ultimate triumph of God's purpose. Though this sense of triumph was often phrased in terms of victorious battle and the enslavement of hostile nations, a deeper spiritual perception was that if such a triumph was to occur at all, it would be a spiritual triumph in a very different—a "new"—creation. As we read the Hebrew Bible—what Christians call the Old Testament—we see a struggle between nationalistic and rather vindictive views of God and a very different view of God as a being of love, mercy, and compassion. In some prophetic passages, and very clearly in Jesus, the compassionate view totally replaces the vindictive view, and a universal concern for creation replaces a nationalistic concern for the restoration of the monarchy to Israel.

Biblical texts like Hosea 6:2 ("after two days he will revive us; on the third day he will raise us up"), though originally referring to the vindication

11. Plato, *The Republic*, Book 2, 362a.

of Israel in face of her political enemies, could have engendered in Jesus the idea of a personal raising from death. That would become a symbol for some sort of vindication of Jesus' ministry, signifying that it would not simply end with failure and death, but would somehow live on in the lives of the Jesus community. It would hardly have been conceived as a global and universally observable event, and whether or not it would usher in the final fulfilment of God's purpose for creation might have been unclear. After all, even in Jesus' day, such a final fulfilment would have to include the whole world. Once the idea of a national triumph for the state of Israel had been given up, a spiritual interpretation of a "Davidic monarchy" would have to include a realistic concern for the whole gentile world. Indeed, it would have to include the whole cosmos, though Jesus could have had no idea of the vast extent of that cosmos. It seems more likely that Jesus, whose concern during his very short teaching life was only with the renewal of Israel, foresaw the growth of a world-wide community that would be oriented towards an unknown final goal of the union of all things with God. But the prophetic symbolism of an ultimate victory continued, as with the earlier prophets, to be fused with hopes of more local and transient movements of judgment and renewal in a specific historical community. This was a well-established feature of prophetic discourse, combining a hope for an ultimately full future union with God with a more limited hope of better times to come in the historically not too distant future.

Thus, I do not find it hard to suppose that Jesus could well have thought that he would continue to be present "with" this community in some fashion. He is reported to have said that the high priest would see the "Son of Man" coming in the power of God,[12] and that is consistent with a belief that Jesus would appear, at least to his disciples, fully existent and united to the glory of God, after his death. A fervent belief that he would live with God and that his union with God would become widely known in some way certainly seems to be a plausible belief for Jesus to have had.

Again, I am not probing the secrets of Jesus' mind, or trying to suggest that we can know as historians what Jesus believed. I am trying to think what it would have been comprehensible for Jesus to believe, given an acceptance of his Jewish tradition, allowing that he could have had a sense of his unique experience of the presence and guidance of God, and also a belief in his calling to criticize and transform his religious tradition. This thought-experiment might make plausible the sort of interpretation of the

12 Matt 26:64.

parables I am suggesting, which is very different from taking him to be a failed apocalyptic prophet, a moral teacher, a social revolutionary, or a judgmental prophet of doom and destruction.

I am suggesting that such differences of interpretation spring from different assessments of the general authenticity of the Jewish prophetic tradition, of what constitutes real spiritual insight (which for me would involve a concern for universal welfare and cooperative and self-sacrificial loving relationships), and of what is thought to be possible for a human being who is attuned to the spiritual world in an extraordinary but still fully and properly human way. Jesus is supremely a Spirit person, standing in the Jewish stream of religious thought, which for many of us expresses the most adequate view of spiritual reality available, though it is most certainly still capable of further development. As such, he can plausibly be seen as the embodiment in one era of historical time of supreme and eternal Wisdom, and as the mediator of Spirit to a new spiritual community that has the vocation of leading to the union of all things in God.

JESUS AND THE KINGDOM OF GOD

If Jesus was the embodiment of divine Wisdom in a human person, then his teachings are of enduring significance for all human lives. If this teaching, as recorded in the Synoptic Gospels, is largely expressed in parables, then it is important to try to grasp what the parables are saying. It is generally agreed that the parables are centred on the idea of the "kingdom (the rule, *basileia*) of God," so it is important to gain some understanding of what is meant by this.

Jesus said, "The kingdom of God is among/within (*entos*) you."[13] Whether the word *entos* should be translated as "within" or "among," in both cases the kingdom is *a present reality*, not just a future hope. God rules as hearts are united to God in love. This idea was not foreign to the Judaism of Jesus' day. Indeed, it is the heart of Judaism. Jesus is the exemplary Jew; in him Judaism is revealed in its true spiritual depth. Yet Jesus definitively rejected any nationalistic and political aspirations, which were sometimes found in the prophetic writings, and taught that the God of Abraham and Isaac was to be seen as a God of universal and unlimited love, and all beings were to be united and transfigured in the divine life, to become sharers in the divine nature. In this way, Judaism might find the fulfilment of its

13. Luke 17:21.

vocation, becoming a truly world-wide faith which would culminate in the "marriage," the intimate union, of all humanity and the divine life.

If all this is true, then it becomes plausible to say that in Jesus the rule of God had come close. If we have a sense of the progressive revelation of God in the Abrahamic tradition and of the charismatic personality of Jesus, it becomes comprehensible to believe that Jesus was the King of this "kingdom of God," in the sense that God ruled in his human life completely and without reserve. This, if it was true, was certainly a major breakthrough in the history of humanity, especially in the Jewish tradition in which he was brought up and of which he was part.

The God of Abraham and Isaac had been clearly seen, by the time of the great sixth century BCE prophets, to be the one and only creator of all things other than itself. This was a God of mercy, and of compassion. But it was also often thought of as a God of strict justice, who had not hesitated to kill millions of people when they offended the divine standards. That God would one day, it was widely thought, take revenge on the historic enemies of Israel and subject them to the rule of the descendants of Abraham.[14]

It was thought by some that there was an immense gulf between God, high and lifted up above the whole of creation, and the mass of humanity, which could only bow down and adore the divine majesty and humble itself before throne of God. Only by strict obedience to the Torah, the law of God, could people be sure of being accounted worthy to stand in the presence of God.

The idea of a life beyond this world was widely accepted, but it was not central to Jewish belief. Many of the most orthodox denied it, and it was conceived in very different ways, perhaps only as desirable to very few great saints, and otherwise as a rather gloomy and ephemeral world of the dead.

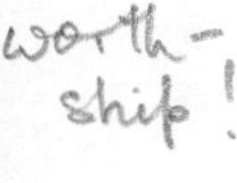

Jewish thought, recorded in the Hebrew Bible, brought to the world, slowly developed over many centuries, the idea of one Creator who had a moral purpose for the world. Value, especially moral value, and purpose, were central to the created order. But to some extent the more ancient idea of God as giving the moral law only to the people of the twelve tribes, of requiring strict obedience, which could be attained by only an elite few, of punishing them ruthlessly for any disobedience, and of having as a goal the triumph of Israel as a political kingdom, by means of violent conflict, remained in place.

14. "[T]he clans of Judah . . . shall devour to the right and to the left all the surrounding peoples" (Zech 12:6).

Jesus inherited this religious tradition, and it could be said that he represented it at its best. But, according to the Gospels, he also severely criticized these leftovers of ancient belief, and any attitude that made correct religious observance the final test of spiritual attainment. He also seemed to assume a more direct spiritual authority than that of the official theologians and leaders of the Jewish priestly establishment, and spoke in original and striking terms of a God who cared for the poor and even for those who were worldly and selfish. Jesus' God was a God of unlimited care for the welfare of creatures, who was concerned to heal sickness, forgive those who had been evil, and ultimately unite all people without exception to the divine nature.

It is plausible to hold that, in his parables, Jesus teaches about such a God, and in his life, he shows what a life ruled by God, a life that embodies in a human form the divine nature and presence, is like. It becomes plausible to think that as a King he founds a kingdom, a society in which the divine presence continues to exist. Jesus will rule this kingdom for ever, and he becomes the one who will place the divine rule that was in him within the hearts of men and women. He "baptizes with the Spirit"; he is the medium of Spirit to his disciples. Thus, a new bond between humans and the divine is established, by which God lives and acts in them, and they become, as he was, sharers in the divine life.

This was a new understanding of the relation between humanity and divinity, between time and eternity. It can be seen, it is seen by some, as a fulfilment of the Jewish tradition. It may also be an important part of the fulfilment of the religious aspirations of the whole of humanity.

But it is vital to bear in mind two things. First, *it is an imperfect and ambiguous fulfilment*, for it does not instantly and completely change human lives to become embodiments of divinity. It is the beginning of a process of transformation that is to continue beyond this life. Its completion lies in a spiritual realm beyond our spacetime, when all things will be united in God.

Second, *it is not a political fulfilment*. The Spirit community is not meant to dominate the world as a supreme institutional power. As Jesus constantly taught, anyone who would lead must be one who serves.[15] The new society, the universal and spiritual union of the disciples of Christ, is to be the servant of all in love, not the ruler of all in authority and power. The

15. Luke 22:26.

Christian churches have found these two things a hard lesson to learn, and it cannot be said that they have learned it very well.

The kingdom of God is present, but not yet in its fullness. It is the seed of what is to come, but it cannot be identified with any actual power or institution. It grows secretly in the hearts of men and women, but it will take many ages for it to become complete. When it is complete, it will gather all creation into that supreme spiritual reality that is the Word of God, the eternal Christ.

MODERN INTERPRETATIONS OF THE PARABLES

That is the general background to my view of the parables. Modern critical treatments of the parables, incorporating greater knowledge of the linguistic structures and historical contexts of their composition, is usually said to have begun in the late nineteenth century with the work of Adolph Jülicher. Following him, C. H. Dodd and Joachim Jeremias wrote influential works that concentrated attention on the fact that the parables spoke of the kingdom of God as a present, not just a future, reality (the Greek text says that the kingdom "has come near," which may be taken to imply something about the past and present, not the future). I shall in this section briefly expound what they say, and try to make clear where my interpretation differs somewhat from theirs. In the section after this, I turn to the work of Dominic Crossan and Bernard Scott, who represent a more revisionist approach that attempts to examine the structure of the parables without theological presuppositions. I examine these interpretations at some length, because I think they do not really avoid important theological presuppositions, and because my presuppositions (as set out in previous sections) are rather different to theirs. To what extent this will turn out to be important remains to be seen. But their work certainly cannot be ignored, and it has contributed considerably to my own understanding. Before turning to a study of the parables themselves, I shall then present the factors that have governed my own presentation of the meaning of the parables.

There have of course been a great many more books and articles published on the parables of Jesus since the seminal works of the four scholars I will deal with. A fairly exhaustive account of many of them can be found in Klyne Snodgrass's book, *Stories with Intent*, especially the second edition (2018), in which he has considered the works of many more recent commentators. I agree with Snodgrass's main point that the parables of Jesus are about the in-breaking of the kingdom of God, and about challenging Jesus' hearers to accept that kingdom. Snodgrass takes full account of the narrative structures, linguistic usages, socio-historical background, the use of stock metaphors, and many very varied receptions and interpretations of the parables. His exposition of the parables is so impressive and comprehensive that I see little point in trying to do a similar thing myself.

My aim is the much more limited one of developing a fully theological account of the parables as expressing the teachings of a person who was the human embodiment of divine Wisdom, disclosing a cosmic purpose for the universe, and inaugurating a new community of life in the Spirit. For this purpose, the work of C. H. Dodd and Joachim Jeremias is important as establishing the view that the kingdom had become present in the person of Jesus. Dominic Crossan and Bernard Scott typify a very different view, and consequently a different way of interpreting the parables, which was to become a feature of many more recent studies of the parables. I want to take that view seriously, but it is not my purpose to explore its many variants in more recent work, some of which eliminate any reference to a transcendent God, concentrating instead on the often puzzling, counter-intuitive, social and moral teachings they find in the parables, primarily criticizing the oppression of the poor and the injustices of the wealthy, and calling for a non-violent but more equitable sharing of the world's goods.

I think the two general approaches I shall explore characterize the main and most important division between modern interpretations of the parables. That division is clearly found, and it can be said to have definitively begun, in the writings of Dodd, Jeremias, Crossan, and Scott, and my case can be made succinctly by paying attention to them, without implying that there is not much later interesting material on these topics. There is, but not for me, and not in this book!

Adolph Jülicher is often taken to have begun modern interpretations of the parables. He objected to traditional interpretations of the parables as allegories, in which each element of a parable was taken to represent some spiritual truth. Instead, he insisted that each parable was making only one salient point, though that point did convey some general principle that was of universal importance, like (one of his examples) "always sacrifice lesser to greater goods." Parables are pictorial representations of general moral principles.

Such a general distinction between parables and allegories does not seem to me to be helpful. The *Oxford English Dictionary* defines an allegory as "a narrative description of a subject under the guise of another, having points of correspondence with its symbolic representation." A religious allegory will describe in everyday down-to-earth forms a spiritual reality. It describes a spiritual truth in terms of natural human events. There may be many or few "points of correspondence" between the spiritual and the natural. Under this definition, parables simply are allegories, even if they only have one point of comparison.

But do parables have only one point of comparison? When, for instance, a parable speaks of a sower scattering seeds, the sower stands for something else, perhaps a preacher or prophet, or perhaps Jesus himself. Different sorts of soil stand for different sorts of people. And the mature "fruits" stand for some sort of desirable and bountiful outcome. Here there are at least three points of comparison, without which the parable is pointless.

Why should anyone insist that a parable should have only one comparison? I suppose Jülicher's point is that one should beware of trying to give a meaning to every detail in Jesus' parables. It is better to see Jesus as making just one main point in each parable, and filling that point out with details that do not necessarily have significance in themselves. When one reads some of Augustine's interpretations of the parables, which are strained and fantastic in the extreme, one can easily appreciate this point. On the other hand, it seems equally extreme to only allow Jesus to make one point of comparison in each parable.

What would be the one point, for example, of the Sower parable? Perhaps the disciples were not sure, which is why they wanted an explanation. Clearly, it is not just about a farmer sowing seeds. A lot of the seeds produce no crop, but a few, finding good soil, produce an abundant crop. This does seem to be about various responses to a teaching, only some of which are positive, but those few are very fruitful.

The trouble with this is that it seems to suggest only a very general point, which would apply to any teaching whatsoever. The parable would be just illustrating one general principle, very familiar to any teacher, that not many people will listen to what one says, but it might be worth going on teaching for the sake of the few who will take it to heart. This is pretty obvious anyway. Why put it into a memorable parable?

The Welsh New Testament scholar C. H. Dodd, accepting Jülicher's distinction between parables and allegories, adds another requirement to make something into a significant parable. Dodd suggests that a parable "has the character of an argument,"[16] and is intended to lead its hearers to make a judgment, and then apply that judgment to the particular situation they are in. He argues that the disciples were in a situation that faced an imminent and catastrophic crisis. They had to see the parable not as a general principle for everyone but as being particularly addressed to them. To do this, they had to see, for instance, that the sower was Jesus, the seed was the message that the kingdom of God had come near, and they should not be discouraged if only a few accepted what they said, for that few (the good soil) would "bear fruit," which must mean something about living a new, productive, richer life in the kingdom.

This, says Professor Dodd, is not a general point, like saying that whenever you teach anything, only a few people will really listen to what you say. It is a specific point about the message of the kingdom of God, which will, if accepted, bring eternal life, even if it is widely rejected by most people. Therefore, proclaiming the kingdom is supremely worth the effort. That is the judgment the disciples are expected to make, and the application is for them to proclaim the kingdom with renewed vigor. I would think, however, that to make that specific point you need to have at least four allegorical points of comparison—the sower, the seed, the soil, and the fruits.

That means that the allegorical explanation of the parable, which all the Synoptic Gospels add to it,[17] is more or less correct. Largely on linguistic grounds, scholars agree that the allegorical explanation given in the Gospels when Jesus was asked what it meant is not, in its precise form, original with Jesus. It is, however, wholly consistent with the original meaning of the parable, and it supports resisting the neat distinction between parables and allegories.

The upshot is that it is reasonable to warn against giving too many fantastical interpretations of every element of parable stories. Nevertheless, there are allegories present, they are susceptible of a variety of interpretations, they may make more than one point, and they are not all about rousing the disciples to vigorous action in view of an impending world-shaking catastrophe. Indeed, my view is that the Parable of the Sower is more suggestive of Jesus as a teacher of wisdom than as a warner of a severe and imminent crisis. That is to say, Jesus is teaching that the rule of God is present in him, and that the response to him will bring a division between those who are open to spiritual insights and those who are more concerned

16. Dodd, *Parables of the Kingdom*, 21.

17. Mark 4:13–20; Matt 13:18–23; Luke 8:11–15.

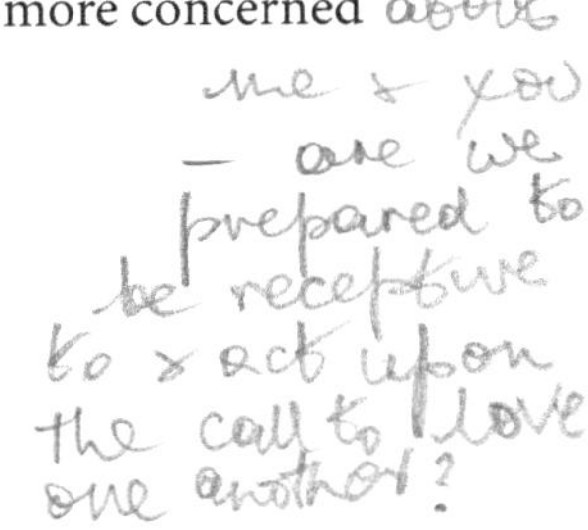

with worldly goals and desires. Those who accept and take to heart what he says will have a share in eternal life, while those who do not will, at least for the present, continue on what they cannot yet see is a way of death.

This could be seen as a sort of crisis, but the crisis is not the advent of a great tribulation and persecution, or possibly (though Dodd certainly does not think this) even the end of the world. It is rather the much more positive offer of the rule of the Spirit, which is the way of more abundant life, through following Jesus. The point of the parable, in other words, is not the need to endure in face of disappointment. The point is to emphasize the promise of the abundant fruits of the Spirit in the lives of those who respond to Jesus. To accept this promise will require personal courage and a renunciation of the pursuit of wealth and worldly cares. But its reward is a life that shares in eternity. This is a present life, and not a deferred hope for some future state.

Professor Dodd believed that there will be no future *parousia*, no historical return of the risen Jesus, though he did think there could be a supra-historical "appearing of Christ in glory." He is best known for espousing a "realized eschatology," that is, for asserting that in Jesus the kingdom is *already present*, and that with Jesus' death and resurrection the glory of God has been truly and finally shown in time. While I am very much in sympathy with the claim that the kingdom is a present reality, not just a future hope, it seems to me that Jesus' death and resurrection is not, taken alone and without a future appearance in glory and a consummation of all things, a sufficient manifestation of the good news that Jesus proclaimed.

Joachim Jeremias, while accepting much of Dodd's analysis, seems to differ in that he thinks that there will be a historical appearing of Christ in glory, and that Jesus expected God to intervene very soon in a catastrophic crisis that would be terrifying for unbelievers, although joyful for disciples of Jesus. He came to express his view as one of "eschatology in process of realization," inaugurated in Jesus yet still to come in its fullness in future history. Jeremias goes on to spell out a difference between Jesus' original teaching in the parables and how the early church later re-interpreted that teaching. In his original teaching, Jesus issued challenges, warnings, and promises to his hearers, saying to them that they were facing an imminent crisis, one that was "the turning point of history,"[18] when all people would be harshly judged by God. Later, when the Gospels were written, Jesus had died, and the parables were re-shaped to explain the apparent delay in his

18. Jeremias, *Rediscovering the Parables*, 33.

final appearance in glory. The whole emphasis changed from warning the crowds of a decisive act of God in history to advice to Christians on how to live, in view of a coming return of Christ, the time of which was unknown. Jeremias admits that this was only a change of emphasis. Nevertheless, he says, it "transformed Jesus into a teacher of wisdom."[19] I shall argue, by contrast, that it would be a mistake to look for a return of Jesus within our historical time or in this unreconstructed universe, and that Jesus always was a teacher of wisdom, attempting, as John's Gospel suggests strongly, to teach an enduring spiritual wisdom that was meant to be developed and known throughout the world.

Dodd and Jeremias accept that one must examine closely the linguistic structures that we find in what are often heavily edited parables, as well as the historical context in which they were originally spoken. They emphasize that the parables were largely about the kingdom of God, and represent the kingdom as being in some sense already present in Jesus. They both reject interpretations that see the kingdom purely as some cosmic catastrophe that is yet to come, but that will happen in the near future. Yet they are both suspicious of what they call "theological" interpretations, which read rather grandiose doctrines about the origin and goal of the universe into the parables. I hope to show that just such a "grandiose" doctrine is present in the parables, though it can (obviously) easily be missed.

REVISIONIST INTERPRETATIONS OF THE PARABLES

Dominic Crossan and Bernard Scott agree that Jesus' talk about the kingdom of God is about a present reality, but go much further, and deny that Jesus was concerned with a future purpose at all. Talk of the kingdom was, they claim, used by Jesus to subvert ordinary expectations and conventional social relations, and to provide a new way of seeing human existence and a new set of radically egalitarian and non-violent values. There is no perfect future to hope for, but there is the possibility of authentic living in this one ambiguous world in which we live. I think this view helpfully shifts the focus of the parables from historical expectation of the miraculous to present experience of the spiritual dimension of human existence. At the same time, it could end in denying the existence of a real spiritual dimension and goal altogether, in which case I believe it provides an illuminating but ultimately diminished analysis of the parables.

19. Jeremias, *Rediscovering the Parables*, 87.

There will not be a further return of Christ in history. That is to say, the kingdom does not come with an imminent and violent act of God in history. It is a society of non-violence, and it exists now insofar as people enter it by their own action, though such action can be seen as a collaboration with God. Crossan rules out the possibility that there will ever actually exist a time when the kingdom exists in its fullness, and when evil has been fully overcome. He writes, "Jesus proclaimed non-violent resistance to the injustice of Roman imperialism in a world that belonged to a just and non-violent God."[20]

Jesus, according to Crossan, brought about a paradigm shift in traditional Jewish thought, by stressing God's non-violence, the need for active cooperation with God, and the religious demand to subvert the hierarchical and oppressive social systems of his day. He was not a proclaimer of a future perfected society or of a sudden ending of history by a terrifying divine act. Nor did he positively teach by giving examples of how to live a truly spiritual life. His parables challenge "the absolutes of our religious faith, the certainties of our theological vision," and the prejudices of our social traditions. Jesus' intention is to raise consciousness, to provoke debate, to "shake the foundations of our world." He is in favor of "permanent questioning," not of laying down enduring moral or religious principles.

Crossan envisages what he calls "permanent eschatology," which is not either a realized, present kingdom (Dodd), or a future historical kingdom (Jeremias), but is the present shattering and ending of our "old world" of values, plans, and expectations, and the advent of a "new world" of risk, uncertainty, and openness to the future. This new world can only be described in parables, poetic metaphors, which radically reverse our ordinary values and replace them with something that cannot be expressed except in the parables themselves. He quotes with approval some words of D. J. Hawkin: "a new scheme of things, in which ordinary values are reversed and reasonable judgments disqualified."[21]

As examples, he takes the Parable of the Good Samaritan to be, not an example of good behavior (though Luke makes it so), but an overturning of previous views of who is good (Jews) and who is bad (Samaritans). The Parable of the Prodigal Son is not about welcoming back a penitent, but about seeing a waster feasting while a dutiful son is ignored. The Parable of

20. Crossan, *Power of Parable,* ch. 6.

21. Crossan, *Power of Parable,* 78.

the Pharisee and the Publican sees a good man as rejected and a bad man as accepted. Our ordinary values are overturned.

Despite the close textual analyses that he provides, he still seems to be appealing to what Jesus "originally intended," which is hardly possible to ascertain just from a study of the text. It turns out that Jesus' original intention (to reverse, undermine, and evoke a new way of seeing the experienced world) is remarkably similar to a Wittgenstein-influenced analysis of religious language as non-referential, but as comprising a distinctive "language-game" and form of life, which resists translation into allegorical or factual statements. Crossan suggests that the longing for immortality, for instance, is "idolatrous," a misplaced factual expectation. It should be replaced by an acceptance that some ways of life are of eternal significance in the present, even though there is no existence beyond physical death.

There is indeed a sense in which Jesus reverses some ordinary values. But this is far from being a reversal in which the very notions of good and bad are put in question, and morality itself is subverted. It is a re-adjustment of our notions of good and bad, but with a heavily stressed insistence on an absolute and crucial difference between them. Jesus says that we must not be angry or swear on oath or take revenge; these are absolute and binding moral values, though what exactly they imply for our everyday conduct is hard to work out. What is castigated is prejudiced hatred of Samaritans, or attitudes of resentment, or pride in one's religious or moral superiority. It is simply not true that ordinary values (that is, what we all really know to be binding, though we may repress the knowledge) are reversed. It is even less true that "reasonable judgments are disqualified." It is the "wisdom of the world"—that is, the valuing of wealth and power and privilege—that is criticized, in favor of the wisdom of God, which consists in understanding how best to care for others, and for the world that is God's gift to humanity.

I would be seriously upset if I thought that Jesus' message was one of undermining ordinary moral values and rational discourse. Indeed, I would regard this as a potentially corrupting teaching, though that is far from what Crossan wants. He apparently thinks of ordinary moral reasoning as inherently defective, and in need of being reversed. Whereas I think that ordinary moral reasoning is just what is needed, though it is often corrupted by self-interest and a lack of the ability to see things from an impartial (from God's!) point of view.

There is a philosophical underpinning of views like Crossan's, which does not derive from the parables themselves, but from the radically post-modern belief that religious language has no objective ontological referent, but instead outlines a distinctive form of life that is not subject to external criticism. There is no objectively existing God, whose causal influence on the world makes a difference to what happens. There is no life beyond physical death, and there is no future elimination of evil to be expected. Moral language, similarly, does not pretend to state objective truths that might be rationally supported. "The logic of ethics is undermined by the mystery of God," writes Crossan.[22] I think this is apt to lead to moral anarchy, and leaves us without any reasonable way of even understanding what it means to say that God is good. After all, Satanists, too, can shatter the complacency of our moral world, reverse our moral values, and open up uncharted paths into the future. Without reason and morality, "man's abode in Being," of which Heidegger was so fond, can be an opening onto an abyss of amoral and irrational absurdity. In contrast, an insistence on the objective and actual existence of truth, beauty, and goodness is the presupposition of Jesus' life and teaching. Jesus does not subvert this, but points out how far from understanding it human beings are.

Jesus would be right to state that both Roman imperialist occupation and the prudish self-righteousness of many religious believers block the way to accepting the rule of God. But does it seem accurate to suggest that he was offering non-violent resistance to the Romans? Even if he was, could he at the same time really just be interested in challenging people to think for themselves? Many people did, after all, favor Roman ways of ordering society. Crossan is aware of this paradox, but he argues that Jesus' method of challenging accepted views is in fact the most appropriate way to get people, or at least to get Galilean peasants, to become conscious of their own situation of oppression and inequality. The parables present a "pedagogy of the oppressed," contrasting the hierarchies of society with the radical social levelling demanded by God's kingdom of justice. They do not have to present a positive doctrine; it is enough to start a debate about justice.

An explicit comparison with Socrates is made, whose teachings were later made into doctrines by his disciples, but whose intention was actually to query all old certainties. It seems to me, however, that one major difference between Socrates and Jesus is this: it seems highly likely that Jesus was a Jew who accepted the Torah as a way of life revealed by God. For such a person, the idea of divine revelation could not be rejected, though its interpretation could certainly be questioned. Socrates accepted no revelation,

22. Crossan, *Power of Parable*, 82.

and he had no revelation to interpret, no God to question. Jesus certainly reformulates the wisdom traditions of Jewish faith and the wilder shores of apocalyptic literature, but he does not wholly abandon them. He drives deeper, as in the antitheses in the Sermon on the Mount, when he expands "Do not kill" to "Do not be angry."[23] He does the same with the imagery of the "Day of the Lord," when he turns the divine judgment on evil against Israel itself, as the prophet Amos before him had done (Amos 5:18). He reformulates the idea of the Messiah from being a warrior who leads Israel to victory, to being a prince of peace and a liberator of humanity as a whole from sin. He does say that God's kingdom is present, that it comes without violence, and that it requires human moral commitment. But does he say that it is a form of non-violent resistance to Roman imperialism?

Jesus is never recorded as criticizing Roman rule, though he often criticizes Jewish religious leaders. If Jesus' parables have political significance, that has to be read into them; it is not present in the text. Jesus' teachings do have social and ethical implications, but those are not just to do with resistance to Rome or imperialist governments. They are to do with constructing a society in which the weak will be cared for and concern for the well-being of all is a divine command. But that political concern is not the primary thing, and Jesus hardly, if ever, speaks overtly of the political situation of his day. The great alienation is not just political oppression. It is estrangement from God, the supremely wise, beautiful, and loving Source of all. The gospel is about achieving union with God, and so sharing in the divine nature.

Crossan insists that the kingdom of God is present, not future; that it is collaborative, not a cataclysmic divine act; and that it is non-violent, not a final armed conflict. This is true, but it needs some qualification. The kingdom *is* present, but *not yet in its fullness*. The kingdom *is* collaborative, but it is the active and transforming *power of the Spirit* that enables human collaboration to be effective. The kingdom *is* non-violent, but it is more than that, it is *the fullness of wisdom, joy, and love*, which can transform human lives even in conditions of political oppression.

Crossan is in danger of replacing such a spiritual intention (to know and love God) with a political intention (to resist imperial rule). How does he know, anyway, what Jesus' intentions in telling parables were? By using his imagination, instructed by an informed but still speculative idea of what Galilean peasants were, in his opinion, likely to be thinking. This attempt

23. Matt 5:21–26.

to understand the intentions of Jesus is even more speculative than some of the older quests to uncover the historical Jesus, if only because intentions are harder to uncover than publicly observable actions. It is in any case rather odd for a writer heavily influenced by structuralism to try to guess at a writer's intentions. After all, a main thesis of structuralism is to say that the intentions of authors are irrelevant to the structure of a text.

There is an ideology working underneath this sort of approach. It is that Jesus is a Galilean peasant who was not the divine Wisdom incarnate, but was a subverter of the social order in which he lived. This is better than thinking that Jesus was a failed prophet of the end of the world. But it says little about God, creation, or redemption. For Crossan, there is no such "grand narrative," which many modern philosophers think to be obsolete! But what if Jesus had a grand narrative, and it was given by the Jewish tradition, and by his belief that he was a human embodiment of the divine Wisdom that ordered the world towards a finally overwhelming goodness?

Bernard Scott, like Crossan, does not think there is much hope of getting to the original words of Jesus, and agrees that parables are essentially polyvalent. They have no one rigid meaning. He says "A parable's richness cannot be exhausted."[24] This is a valuable insight. But his positive account of parables is governed by an underlying belief about the status and role of Jesus. As in Crossan, parables are presented as speech-acts that have the function of subverting established views. They challenge all "insider-outsider" distinctions, and evoke a sense of God's "radical solidarity" with common folk, in all their everydayness, uncleanness (breaking rules of ritual purity), and lack of spectacular miracles. They "redescribe reality," imparting new ways of seeing the world, but these redescriptions are not translatable into secret or fantastic theological or philosophical doctrines. "Jesus was both anti-wisdom and anti-apocalyptic," says Scott.[25] The way of wisdom, according to him, is the fantasy of a perfect life in the world, in which goodness is rewarded and evil punished; the way of apocalypse is the fantasy of a golden future. Parables, he says, deny both ways; they subvert the myths that make life bearable by offering fantasies. In place of such fantasies, what do parables offer? Surprises, shocks, acceptance of the mixture of tragedy and heroism that is human life, a radical acceptance of life as it is, with a belief that God is present precisely in that ambiguity.

24. Scott, *Hear Then the Parable*, Preface, Kindle loc 35.

25. Scott, *Hear Then the Parable*, Epilogue, Kindle loc 5904.

The difficulty for this view is that the parables do seem to speak of a golden future, the kingdom of God. And they speak of the way to share in that future, the true wisdom of living in a way that leads to the kingdom. It seems unduly reductive to suggest that the radical good news that Jesus proclaims does not give hope for a future life with God, and does not speak of a decisive judgment on evil and a triumph of love that will eliminate the ambiguities of the everyday. However, we may do well to listen to the ambiguities of the texts that Crossan and Scott bring out so well, and also to their interpretation of the parables as teaching the solidarity of God with all people without exception, a teaching that subverts usual expectations of human hierarchies and relationships.

AN EXPANSIVE INTERPRETATION OF THE PARABLES

In this text, I aim to state a view of Jesus' teaching, as expressed in his many parables, which I can now put quite briefly, and work out progressively as I consider some parables in more detail. I believe that Jesus taught a non-violent and non-exclusive view of God as a being of unrestricted and universal love, who was especially concerned with the reconciliation of those who were alienated in some way from knowledge and love of God ("God was in Christ reconciling the world to himself").[26] Nothing in all creation can limit God's reconciling love ("I am convinced that . . . not anything in all creation will be able to separate us from the love of God in Christ Jesus our Lord").[27] The primary purpose of God's manifestation in Jesus was to enable all things in heaven and earth to share in the divine nature ("He [God] has made known to us the mystery of his will . . . to gather up all things in him, things in heaven and things on earth").[28] I suppose this might be called a "spiritual eschatology," a belief that there will be a future state of a life in union with God, but that it will be not in this physical universe, but in a transfigured, spiritual cosmos.

My aim in considering the parables is to argue for this belief, particularly in view of the fact that such an aim is often thought to be unreasonable or even impossible. I will rely to a great extent on the work of Dodd and Jeremias, though I will offer a much more explicitly theological and cosmically oriented interpretation of the parables I consider. While this will issue

26. 2 Cor 5:19.

27. Rom 8:39.

28. Eph 1:10.

in a very different overall account to that given by Crossan and Scott, I accept that I need to take account of the fact, to which they have drawn attention, that the parables, as set out in the Gospels, contain some passages that have given rise to major misunderstandings of Jesus' message, because, taken in isolation, they can evoke vindictive, exclusive, and judgemental understandings of God. I hope to show that, when seen in the fuller context of Christian discipleship, the dominant note of the parables is one of joy, compassion, and hope. They convey overwhelmingly good news for all, not everlasting torture for some. The meaning they convey, partly hidden, is spelled out more explicitly in John's Gospel.

I particularly need to provide some plausible account of New Testament teachings concerning Jesus' "coming in glory" and the Last Judgment. There is a wide range of views about these matters, and I take the view that talk about a coming great tribulation and a literal return of Christ to earth are dramatic symbols of the ultimate fulfilment of God's purpose for the universe and the elimination of evil from creation. As such, they do not predict specific future historical events, but refer to the assumption of historical events into a spiritual realm, which is a genuinely real sphere of existence, though it transcends literal description. I think such a conception is central to Jesus' teaching, that it can be found in the parables, and that it is made explicit in John's Gospel and some of the New Testament letters.

Jesus' parables were originally almost certainly spoken in Aramaic, and we have them only in Greek versions. The parables are given in the first three Gospels. They exist in slightly different versions in each Gospel. They are placed in different contexts, and linked to various sayings that are put in different places in the different Gospels. The links are often quite obscure, and most scholars think that the parables have been edited and added to in various ways by the editors who collected them from various oral traditions in different early Christian groups.

This may sound a bit negative. But it is very important to know that we do not have perfect and unaltered versions of exactly what Jesus said. We do, however, have good reason to think that we have accurate, even if slightly differing, accounts of his teaching, and we do know what Jesus' followers, within about forty or so years after his death, thought was important about this teaching. What we do know, then, is what the first generation of Christians believed Jesus said, and we also have clues about how they interpreted his sayings. We know the impact Jesus had on some of his followers. But we have to realize that these things were all recorded after they had seen or heard of his death, his resurrection, and the amazing experience of the Spirit at Pentecost, together with experiences of the living Christ in early Christian gatherings. So, there will probably be a certain amount of reading present experiences of the risen Jesus back into the past records of his life. We could say that what we have in the parables is a record (to be exact, three records) of the impact Jesus' teaching had on the early disciples, some idea of the main elements of that teaching as they remembered it, and an idea of the slightly different ways in which some of them interpreted that teaching.

The perspective I am taking is that John's Gospel is a sophisticated and fully worked out version of what the parables were saying in less abstract ways for the Galilean crowds to which Jesus spoke. I also want to show that the form of personal idealism I hold does significantly derive from the biblical records of the life and teaching of Jesus, who is taken to be an authentic disclosure of the nature and purpose of God. What I will do is to set out in a brief but systematic way the major features of one form of Christian personal idealism, and show how the main parables of Jesus, when interpreted expansively, give support to these features. As a corollary, this may illustrate how John's Gospel can be seen as an expansion and reflection on the teachings expressed in the parables, turning cryptic stories into more formalized speeches that spell out the implications of Jesus' brief Galilean ministry for a deeper understanding of the nature and destiny of humanity. The order and grouping of the parables in this book is intended to reflect and support my theological project. It is not meant to replace or compete with more formal classifications of the parables by New Testament scholars from Bultmann onwards.

PART TWO

A Theological Interpretation of the Parables

ONE

The Coming of the Kingdom

One of the most certain things about the teaching of Jesus is that he proclaimed the coming of the "kingdom of God" (*basileia tou Theou*). This can properly be translated as the "rule of God" or even interpreted as the rule of the Spirit of God. I find it helpful to accept that interpretation, because we might say that the teaching is primarily about living a spiritual life, or living in the way of the divine Spirit.

Jesus said that "the time is fulfilled, and the kingdom of God has come near; repent [turn your minds from ambition, fame, greed, and hatred] and believe [trust in the power of God]" (Mark 1:15). If the rule of God has come near, then something new has happened, something recent and something active—it "has come," it has not just been discovered as something that has always been there. It fulfils what the prophets had looked forward to, and it calls for a positive response of trust. But what is it? Strange as it may seem, people have given many different answers to this question, ranging from the idea that the world is coming to an end to the idea that it is a new way of looking at human life. I do not accept either of these answers. But before I give my own view, there is a preliminary question that needs to be addressed. Jesus typically teaches in parables, and an answer to the question about what the "kingdom of God" is can probably be found in Jesus' parables. But *why* does Jesus teach in parables?

HAVE THE PARABLES A HIDDEN SECRET?

When Jesus is asked why he speaks in parables, all the Synoptic Gospels refer to Isaiah chapter 6, verses 9 and 10, where God tells the prophet to speak, but warns that people will not all comprehend or understand him. If they did, the prophecy says, they would turn and be healed, but their eyes are blinded and their ears blocked. There is a warning here, for the prophecy goes on to say that destruction and judgment will come upon those who fail to see or hear the hidden meaning of his message. In its original context, the judgment came with the exile of the Israelites to Babylon and the destruction of Israel as a nation, which was a disaster of major proportions. Such a warning is uncannily appropriate to Jews in the time of Jesus, for the destruction of the Jerusalem Temple and Israel as a nation was not far in the future, and that was certainly a national disaster.

It seems that Jesus was speaking of the coming destruction of Israel, and yet of the possibility of healing and fulfilment for those who hear and trust him. But, as the quotation from Isaiah shows, he speaks in *intentionally obscure* terms so that it takes a special sort of personal response for people to understand what he really means. Such a response is not merely a theoretical assent, because it involves a commitment to turn away from a "worldly" way of life to a spiritual way of life, that is, a way of life in dependence on the Spirit.

We can take this in a rather harsh way, as if God is intentionally blinding most people to the truth, and giving the requisite insight only to a few chosen souls. Such an interpretation makes everything that happens depend solely upon God, who does what God wants with relatively passive human minds, making them either blind or "seeing" in accordance with a purely divine decision.

Dominic Crossan offers a similar but slightly different interpretation.[1] He thinks that in this passage Jesus is seen as threatening punishment on his hearers for their incomprehension. He does this as a revenge punishment for their rejection of him. Because they reject him, they cannot comprehend the parable, and because of that they are punished by being themselves rejected by God. Since Crossan sees that this is totally against the spirit of Jesus, he sees it as a punitive invention of the Gospel editors. His is an ingenious interpretation, but there is no need to take the Gospel teaching thus.

There is a different interpretation, which gives human minds a more active and responsible role. Intellectual understanding and existential decisions about how to live are closely interwoven. The "blind" are those who choose to live a worldly life, while the "seeing" are those who are in some

1. Crossan, *Power of Parable*, ch. 1.

way dissatisfied with themselves and their lives, and are ready to respond positively to calls to a more spiritual life. It is not *God* or *Jesus* who blinds hearers and punishes them. Their blindness is *self-inflicted* by their worldliness or, if they are religious, by their hypocrisy. Their punishment is simply to become what they are making of themselves by their behavior.

When Jesus says, "to him who has, will more be given, and from him who has not, even what he has will be taken away,"[2] this would mean that those with some spiritual understanding will receive more of it, while those who lack spiritual understanding will not receive any. The parables need to be interpreted spiritually, not materially, and they give spiritual insight to those who are ready and eager to receive it.

Professor C. H. Dodd, like Crossan, also holds that this passage about the "mystery" of the parables is not likely to be something that Jesus could have said.[3] Professor Dodd finds it incredible that Jesus could have wanted to make his message obscure. As I look at the teachings of many religious leaders around the world, however, it seems that it is common, almost compulsory, for them to speak in cryptic and puzzling ways, so as to call for a certain sort of response from their hearers, to sort out those who were truly concerned with a spiritual search from those who saw religion, if they regarded it at all, mainly as a prop for their nationalistic or political ambitions. The responses of hearers to the parables would be one that either saw a sort of meaningful spiritual point in what was said or dismissed it as nonsense or absurdity.

Whether or not this passage about the mystery of the parables and the hardness of heart of many hearers can be traced back to the historical Jesus, it makes sense to think that the parables contain a spiritual meaning that would remain obscure or vacuous to those whose hearts were set on the goals of wealth and fame that the world offers.

Another interpretation is offered by Bernard Scott in *Hear Then the Parables*, who sees the parables in general as subverting traditional social and religious traditions. He sees this passage about the "hardening of hearts" as a challenge to Jesus' hearers to make their own decision. That decision is about who is "in" and who is "out" of the kingdom. For, Scott says, it is not at all clear that the disciples themselves are understanding the parables correctly—as their request for an interpretation shows. Jesus is blurring or

2. Mark 4:25, but included by Matthew at this point in his narrative (Matt 13:12).

3. Dodd, *Parables of the Kingdom*, 14f.

challenging or subverting the division between the "good religious" people and the "outsiders."[4]

It does seem to be true that the disciples misunderstood Jesus on many points, as the Gospels themselves repeatedly say. It is also true that Jesus does subvert the belief of many religious traditionalists in their own superior knowledge and piety. The application to modern churches is that no group, whether traditionalist or radical, is justified in drawing a line between themselves and the "outsiders," in saying that only they have the "true faith" while others are infidels. I think the general teachings of Jesus support such an application. Yet it does seem that a clear distinction is being made between those whose "hearts are hardened" and those who bear fruit. While people must be very wary of having a sense of religious "correctness" that excludes everyone else, it is still the case that only some people let the gospel transform their lives in a positive way.

Jesus is certainly not teaching that there is a small religious elite who have a secret understanding of his teaching—that is the gnostic way. But he is teaching that only some people truly understand—that is, let their lives be inwardly transformed by—the gospel. There is a challenge to his hearers, but it is not so much a challenge to make their own minds up, as a challenge to see what it really means to understand and take to heart his teaching. True understanding is, perhaps, not so much to believe the right set of propositions or carry out the right set of religious practices, but to be filled with the spirit of accepting, compassionate, and sacrificial love, which is shown to them by and offered to them in Jesus.

THE SOWER: Jesus as a teacher of wisdom

> Again he began to teach beside the sea. Such a very large crowd gathered around him that he got into a boat on the sea and sat there, while the whole crowd was beside the sea on the land. He began to teach them many things in parables, and in his teaching he said to them: "Listen! A sower went out to sow. And as he sowed, some seed fell on the path, and the birds came and ate it up. Other seed fell on rocky ground, where it did not have much soil, and it sprang up quickly, since it had no depth of soil. And when the sun rose, it was scorched; and since it had no root, it withered away. Other seed fell among thorns, and the thorns grew up and

4. Scott, *Hear Then the Parable*, ch. 17.

> choked it, and it yielded no grain. Other seed fell into good soil and brought forth grain, growing up and increasing and yielding thirty and sixty and a hundredfold." And he said, "Let anyone with ears to hear listen!"
>
> When he was alone, those who were around him along with the twelve asked him about the parables. And he said to them, "To you has been given the secret of the kingdom of God, but for those outside, everything comes in parables; in order that
>
> 'they may indeed look, but not perceive,
> and may indeed listen, but not understand;
> so that they may not turn again and be forgiven.'"
>
> And he said to them, "Do you not understand this parable? Then how will you understand all the parables? The sower sows the word. These are the ones on the path where the word is sown: when they hear, Satan immediately comes and takes away the word that is sown in them. And these are the ones sown on rocky ground: when they hear the word, they immediately receive it with joy. But they have no root, and endure only for a while; then, when trouble or persecution arises on account of the word, immediately they fall away. And others are those sown among the thorns: these are the ones who hear the word, but the cares of the world, and the lure of wealth, and the desire for other things come in and choke the word, and it yields nothing. And these are the ones sown on the good soil: they hear the word and accept it and bear fruit, thirty and sixty and a hundredfold."
>
> —Mark 4:1–26

The Parable of the Sower is the first parable recounted in Mark's Gospel, and it can be seen as making precisely this point about the rule of divine love in the hearts of men and women. The parable, very well known, tells of a sower who sows seeds. Some were eaten by birds, some fell on stony ground, some fell among thorns, which smothered them, and some fell on good soil. Only those in good soil produced fruit, in various degree of richness. C. H. Dodd suggested that originally the details of this parable, about the different kinds of soil and crop, were not significant. Jesus would have been concerned only with the end of the process, which is the production of a fruitful crop (the process itself, Dodd says, probably concerned the Hebrew prophets, who prepared the ground for Jesus, but they lie in the past). He would have been saying that the crop is ready for harvesting, and calling his disciples to go out and reap.[5] The allegorical interpretation, which concentrates on the different types of soil, "generalizes the application" in order to give warning and encouragement to Christians. It is, he suggests, wholly an interpretation by the early church.

Jeremias agrees that the early church interpretation transfers an eschatological emphasis into a psychological one. It is, in his terms, a "contrast-parable." To concentrate on the process of growth is, he says, a Western way of thinking, whereas an "Oriental" thinks only of the contrast between inauspicious beginnings and abundant fruition.[6] Thus, originally Jesus would have been saying that from small beginnings, in the patriarchs and prophets, God has produced a miraculously abundant crop, which is now ready for harvesting. The "eschatological" point is that the kingdom of God has dawned; the crop is ready to be harvested; the judgment is here and now. The "psychological" point would be that, in a possibly long delay before the return of Christ in glory, preachers should not be discouraged if their preaching is often rejected, and that they must beware of persecution and worldliness.

There is, however, something rather odd about this contrast, even apart from the questionable contrast between the "Western" and the "Oriental" mind. When Jeremias seeks to illustrate what the eschatological interpretation is, he says, "in spite of every failure and opposition, God brings from hopeless beginnings the glorious end that he has promised."[7] The disciples must stand firm in face of hostility and desertions from their cause. Yet this is precisely what the allegorical or psychological interpretation says! The only difference is that the allegorical explanation spells this out for subsequent generations of Christians, and warns them not to desert or fall away (which, of course, is also true for those who first heard Jesus preach).

Crossan and Scott take a very different approach. Scott, speaking of the Parable of the Sower, remarks that it is more about failure than success (most of the seeds fail to be fruitful, and the final harvest is pretty ordinary anyway, he says). For him, the allegorical interpretation is an early church construction, and the original point of the parable is that "in failure and in everydayness lies the miracle of God's activity."[8] The kingdom includes the ordinary and the unclean, and calls neither for the "moral perfection of

5. Dodd, *Parables of the Kingdom*, 136.

6. Jeremias, *Rediscovering the Parables*, 117f.

7. Jeremias, *Rediscovering the Parables*, 120.

8. See Scott, *Hear Then the Parable*, ch. 17.

Torah nor the apocalyptic solution of overwhelming harvest." God is in the ordinary everyday ambiguity of life.

This, it seems to me, hardly seems to be particularly good news, and it fails to see the kingdom as something new. His view is, ironically, a sort of wisdom teaching (find God in the ordinary), but God is not doing anything special in Jesus, and Jesus is not fulfilling the demands of Torah or delivering warnings and promises of final judgment and fulfilment. This is so contrary to early Christian faith in Jesus that, despite Scott's close analysis of the structure of the text and of its original historical context, he does not adequately account for the extraordinary explosion of belief in Christ as Lord, except as some sort of primordial mistake.

If the parable is to be a proclamation not of failure but of good news about the dawn of a new age, it must appeal to allegory. The sower must stand for a preacher (and why not Jesus himself, the archetypal preacher of the gospel?); the seed must stand for the gospel, or perhaps for the Holy Spirit; the soil must stand for hearers; and the fruits must stand for some sort of good outcome. Even the eschatological meaning, that the kingdom has dawned, entails that disciples must see the future with hope, be patient, and not despair. In other words, the story has an allegorical meaning, which is intended to elicit an appropriate response.

Many members of the early church did think that there was a delay before Christ's return, so they explicitly drew allegories (like "the sower is Jesus") and moral maxims (like "be hopeful") from the parables. When Jesus taught, he probably did not have such a delay and imminent return in mind. Yet he used allegories (the sower is a preacher) and drew moral conclusions (don't despair), and he surely did not think that the kingdom (the complete rule of God and elimination of all evil) had already come in its fullness. So, there *was* a sort of delay between the presence of the kingdom in its embryonic form and its consummation.

For these reasons, I am rather skeptical of Dodd's and Jeremias's interpretations, mainly because the parable begins with a sower scattering seeds, and seeds grow. There is a lot about growth, and not much about harvesting, in fact harvesting is not even mentioned. It looks as if the stress is after all on the *growth* of seeds, and the reasons for successful or unsuccessful growth, *not* on the harvesting of wheat. There is no reason why this should not reflect an actual situation that Jesus was in, since he was preaching and gathering disciples, and that group was growing, though many ignored or rejected his message. Of course, if one asks about the *sitz in leben*, the setting in life, of Jesus' teaching, we must accept that we are just imagining what it might have been, given our understanding of Jesus. Sometimes such speculation is helpful. For instance, it may seem unlikely that Jesus would have referred to his own "second coming" early in his ministry. But sometimes it borders on fantasy, as when Jeremias suggests that parables about weddings originated in some wedding that Jesus attended, or when Crossan suggests that Jesus' intention was to subvert established prejudices—things we could not possibly know.

Trying to guess the original meaning of the parables is rather like a reversion to old quests for the historical Jesus. We just imagine what Jesus was like, and thus what a person like that in Galilee at that time is likely to have said. Knowledge of the historical context and of the language is very helpful in imagining such things. But it cannot really replace the underlying theological issue of what sort of person Jesus must have been—whether he was an apocalyptic prophet, a questioning philosopher, a charlatan, or an incarnation of the eternal Word and a teacher of spiritual wisdom. I accept the last of these possibilities, and that is bound to affect what one thinks Jesus might have originally said. In the case of the Sower parable, it becomes much more likely that he was concerned with the extent and continuation of his message of the kingdom than with just exhorting the disciples to continue preaching. Naturally he was concerned with both, but there seems little reason to insist that he could not have been using allegories that issued in general maxims about the conditions for fruitful hearing of the message of the kingdom.

THEOLOGICAL INTERLUDE: ON EVIL AND THE DEVIL

It seems, nevertheless, to be generally accepted, largely because of the very different styles of language used, that the explanation of the parable that the Gospels give[9] is not original with Jesus, but is the product of early church reflection upon it. The explanation given in the text is that Jesus gives the good news that God's rule has come near. Some will not hear it at all, and the Synoptic Gospels all say that the "birds" in the parable represent the devil, who wants to stop people being "saved," that is, finding their true lives in union with God.

This mention of the devil raises a general question about the existence of the devil and of evil in a world created by an allegedly good God. This

9. For instance, in Mark 4:13–20.

is such an important question that I feel I should say something about it. What I have to say may seem rather abstract, and I can put my main point very briefly: God wills to create genuinely free and creative societies of persons. God will have to allow them the freedom to hate as well as love, to destroy as well as to create. The devil is a symbol of these tendencies to hate and destruction, which are parts of creation that even God cannot prevent arising. In the end, God's love and wisdom is strong enough to overcome such tendencies, to "overcome the devil." But in the meanwhile, those tendencies just have to exist.

Now for the slightly fuller version. I do not think the devil is some sort of invisible person, just as I do not think that God is just an invisible person. When we think of God, we think of the ultimate and uncreated Source of all beings. There is only one Source of all beings, and that will of course mean that "the devil" exists only because of God. If God is love, as Christians believe, God may necessarily create a world of beings that can express and share God's love. But those beings, as we now know, are products of a universe that develops from a simple initial state (the "Big Bang") through a long process of increasingly organized complexity to the existence of conscious intelligent life-forms. This process involves competition and destruction as well as cooperation and the emergence of new structures and properties. For instance, animals must eat and die, and be subject to general laws of nature, which have to operate regardless of their impact on living things. If we could fully understand the way in which we, as specific sorts of carbon-based intelligent beings, have evolved in accordance with fundamental physical principles, we might see that the basic laws of nature just have to be the way they are if they are to produce beings like us.

If free and intelligent persons are to evolve in a universe like this, the universe would need to possess a high degree of law-like regularity, which would make a stable structure of nature possible, together with an openness and flexibility, which would allow free creativity to emerge. The created cosmos must possess a high degree of both necessity and of freedom, directed by intelligence. That entails that some things have to be the way they are, whether we like it or not, and that some things depend not on our desires but on the free choices of other beings. Either way, it is not possible to have such a universe and for everything in it always to produce nothing but good for all of us. There will have to be things that cause pain and destruction. That is the price of having truly creative, developing, socially interacting intelligent agents.

We can catch a glimpse of how this may be so if we accept that some forms of goodness cannot exist without some possibilities that are in themselves bad. For instance, if one form of goodness is the achievement of excellence in music or sport, that will necessarily involve years of hard training and the overcoming of many difficulties and obstacles. This means that there will be possibilities of failure as well as of success, and there is no way of eliminating those possibilities without eliminating the goods as well. When we learn and make new discoveries in science, in mathematics, in music, painting, and poetry, and in learning to live together with people who are very different from us, there is always the possibility of failure or, more often, of partial success. It may be impossible to have a world containing the possibility of creative success without there also being some possibilities of failure. In a similar way, if loving care for others is a great good, though it often requires a good deal of self-sacrifice, it will be possible to fail to show such care. That may lead to indifference and even to hatred of others who stand in the way of obtaining a great good for oneself.

Probably any world very like ours would have to include many destructive and painful features. But in our world such features have become very much more pronounced than they need have been. The tortures that humans freely inflict on each other in war and violence have made things much worse than they should have been. This is a world in which innocent victims suffer at the hands of the violent. Yet if we are to exist as the sort of beings we are, we may have to come into being in a world like this, where the basic laws can cause destruction as well as open up new creative possibilities for being.

We are far from understanding such basic necessities in nature. How much less could they be understood in biblical times. The fact is that destruction and creation, death and life, success and failure, disease and health, are built into the world created by God. It may be that even God cannot create a world like this unless it contains such polar oppositions. They are built into the structure of created being. Those who believe in God believe that out of this ambiguous world God will bring an overwhelming good. If that was not so, this world would never have been created. If there is a God, if the Source of all beings is overwhelmingly good, then in a world that is yet to come, evil will finally be eliminated and the good things that have been achieved by the struggles of developing creatures in this world will be transfigured and preserved for all to share.

God will ensure that goodness will eventually eliminate evil in any world that God creates. But many of these worlds, including ours, will contain possibilities of chaos and destruction. The idea of the devil represents these possibilities of chaos and destruction as if they were embodied in a person. They are in fact objective features of reality that can tempt human creatures to fall prey to some of the tendencies to chaos and destruction, which are necessarily present in this world that God has created.

God has created a world like this because God has willed to create creatures with creative freedom, who are to realize good things by resolute endeavor. When it is said that the devil tempts people, that means that people can realize their destructive tendencies in order to achieve things that they think are good for themselves. Such tendencies essentially exist as possibilities of their existence. People may simply ignore any message that there is a kingdom, a form of being in which such tendencies will be eliminated. They may ignore the gospel, the message of the ultimate goodness of being, and realize instead the possibilities for egoism and conflict which necessarily exist in the created order.

BACK TO THE SOWER

The Parable of the Sower speaks of such people as those who are tempted by the devil, and ignore the good news of the rule of God. A second group ("the stones") will listen to the gospel message with a sense of initial joy and hope, but when troubles and difficulties come along they fall away. They may come to doubt the possibility of any future existence when an overwhelming good could be realized. They may think the demands of kingdom life are too difficult and unrealistic. They will fall away.

The third group ("the thorns") accept the gospel, but are tempted by the desire for wealth and power, and become filled with worldly cares and desires, and become unfruitful. In our world, in which generations of people have chosen to pursue money and fame, and have taught their children by example to do so as well, it will be very difficult to escape the pull of such "worldly" desires. Attachment to such desires will inevitably end in disillusion and death. In the end, all such desires are doomed to end in failure.

Some seeds, however, bear fruit. The allegorical explanation is that one should respond to the call to enter the kingdom of God whole-heartedly, enduring afflictions and trials, and setting aside delight in wealth and luxury, and then one will live a fulfilled, fruitful life.

This allegorical explanation makes sense. Yet to his disciples Jesus spoke of a secret or mysterious teaching (in Greek, *mysterion*) that the parables partly revealed and partly concealed. What is this mystery?

THE MESSIANIC SECRET

One possibility is that Jesus was preaching a socially revolutionary message, and that the secret is what has been called "the messianic secret" of Mark's Gospel. The secret is that Jesus is the Messiah, the Davidic King, and that the might of Rome will be overthrown by a miraculous divine act. It might indeed have been dangerous to say this overtly to a Galilean crowd, who already chafed at the oppressive rule of Rome and its puppet kings of Judah. But it could have been said privately to an inner group of disciples, who could prepare for this revolutionary event.

Albert Schweitzer thought that Jesus looked for someone else, the "Son of Man," who would come as King, and did not actually claim to be the Messiah himself.[10] It has to be admitted, however, that when the Gospels were written, there was no doubt that the writers believed that Jesus *had* claimed to be the Messiah, though Mark recorded that Jesus told his disciples to keep that claim secret. Even Mark, however, wrote of Jesus entering Jerusalem on a colt with his disciples, while crowds shouted "Blessed is the kingdom of our father David that is coming."[11] This action, calling to mind as it did the prophecy of Zechariah 9:9, would certainly have amounted to a claim to messianic status by Jesus. The response of the crowds to Jesus' arrival implies that they thought the kingdom would be the restoration of a Davidic monarchy in Israel.

Was this, then, the secret behind the parables, that Jesus was the coming King of Israel? It is reasonable to suppose that it was. But *what sort of King* was Jesus to be, and *what sort of kingdom* would he rule? Perhaps the secret is deeper, and is a "mystery" in a more profound and spiritual sense.

To explore this possibility, one has to resort to other New Testament passages, which claim that Jesus is indeed the prophesied Messiah, but that his kingdom is not going to be brought about by revolutionary political action. Before Mark's Gospel was written, the belief was already strongly held

10. Schweitzer, *The Quest of the Historical Jesus.*

11. Mark 11:9.

that Jesus had died on the cross, had appeared after physical death to his disciples, and would return in glory. This strongly suggests that the sower, Jesus, is the "Messiah," the one anointed by God to sow the "word of the kingdom."[12] But the Messiah is not an ordinary earthly ruler of an earthly kingdom. He is the supreme teacher of the fulfilment of God's purpose for human living. God will rule in human lives, and God's rule (the rule of the Spirit) is planted in human lives by Jesus. But it must find "good soil"—a ready acceptance, unmoved by trials and tribulations or by the desire for fame and riches. Humans must work with resolution and endurance to allow God to rule in their lives. If they do, they will "bear fruit." It is not said what that fruit will be, but it is hard not to think of the list of the "fruit of the Spirit" in Galatians 5:22—"love, joy, peace, patience, kindness, generosity, faithfulness, gentleness, and self-control" (the word for "fruit"—*karpos*—is the same in both cases). This letter was almost certainly written before the Gospel of Mark, so the editor of Mark might have known it. Whether or not he did, it is a wonderful list of some main qualities that fulfil the positive potential of human lives for good—both for their own happiness and compassion, and for the well-being of others.

At this level, it becomes plain that hope for the coming of God's kingdom is not just a sort of relatively passive expectation that, one day soon, things will get a lot better. It involves positive action to bring about good, even in an environment that is indifferent or hostile to such action. It is letting the Spirit of self-giving love rule in one's life. It is living by the Spirit, sown and cultivated by Jesus in the heart, and issuing in acts of justice, mercy, compassion, and joy.

This would be an arresting spiritual teaching, and not just an admonition that preachers should not lose heart when they did not make many converts. It is a teaching that casual hearers of the parable might easily miss. If this is so, the interpretation of Jesus as predicting a renewed state of the nation of Israel becomes less appealing. There is a difference between social revolutionaries, angry at present injustices and ready to die to bring about a new sort of political order, and people who try to live by a spirit of self-giving and universal love, whatever present injustices are, or what the possibility of social revolution might be.

There is a hope for a future when good will triumph over evil. But this hope inspires present action for the sake of good, a living dependence on the Spirit of God, a commitment to a spiritual life, putting aside desires for

12. Matt 13:19.

wealth and status, being untroubled by the sorrows and cares of life. The kingdom of God is not just a future state; it is the present rule of Spirit in the hearts of men and women.

THE ULTIMATE SECRET

This thought, however, suggests a further level of mystery in the parable. In the letter to the Ephesians, the writer speaks of the "mystery" (*mysterion* again) revealed in Christ, that God might "gather up all things in him [Christ], things in heaven and things on earth."[13] This is indeed a secret teaching, which is hard to understand, but perhaps the parables speak of it in a veiled way. Jesus is not merely the Messiah, anointed by God to sow the word of a spiritual kingdom, though that is indeed a new teaching, mysterious to many. The greater mystery is that the seed that is sown is *the Spirit*, which is implanted within people's lives, and produces the fruits that result in the lives of those who respond positively. As grain does not exist for itself, but is used as nourishment to feed and build up personal lives, so the fruits of the Spirit are gathered up to feed and build up the community that is to be forever preserved and fulfilled in the being of the eternal Christ.

Such a teaching is more fully spelled out in some New Testament letters and in the Gospel of John. It may be—and has been argued, especially by Adolf von Harnack—that these passages belong to a different, more "mystical" way of thinking about Christ than the more straightforward view of the parables in the Synoptic Gospels. It seems to be true that this way of thinking was more a *reflection* on the nature of Jesus as in some sense divine than a straightforward *memory* of what he actually taught during his life. Yet if one is prepared to say that such reflection brought out into the open a greater truth about Jesus, it is reasonable to think that such truth must in some way have been known to, and taught by, Jesus himself. If the Gospel of John does bring up to the surface a truth about Jesus, one would expect to find at least hints of such truth in Jesus' parables.

To understand the parables in this way, we must see Jesus, as John's Gospel does, as one who embodies the divine in human flesh and blood. That is, as the Word (the *Logos*), which takes human form in Jesus and is mediated through him and by the Spirit to his disciples, bringing the rule of God into human lives. There it progressively conforms those lives, insofar as they accept the Spirit, more closely to the image of God, and the "fruits"

13. Eph 1:10.

are the works of the Spirit in the lives of men and women. In that sense, Christ is in us. This is the new, recent, and active "coming of the kingdom" that Jesus proclaimed. It is the manifestation, in Jesus himself, of the rule of God in human lives, aimed at a final complete union of human and divine, but now present in the person of Jesus.

As Christ works in us, so we are together gathered up 'in Christ," patterned on him and empowered by him, forming one community of beings, in and through which the love of God is manifest on earth. This is the new Israel, not a political state dominating and subduing its enemies, but a spiritual community united in works of love, even love for its enemies, and finding fulfilment in expressing the fruits of the Spirit.

The hope, explicitly expressed in the first chapter of Ephesians, is that "everything in heaven and earth" will find such fulfilment, and will express the being of the eternal Spirit in the life of time. But, for now, those who "live in Christ" are called to be the forerunners of the future destiny to which all are called. Christ calls (sows the word of the kingdom, the community of the Spirit); but many remain enslaved by indifference, anxiety, and desire. Those who hear and respond to the call of Christ are not called to be safe and happy, while everyone else suffers and dies. They are called to "bear fruit," to undertake self-sacrificial action for the welfare of all sentient beings and for the world itself.

That, if much of the rest of the New Testament is to be trusted, is the final mystery of the Parable of the Sower. The one who calls is the one who makes human lives truly fruitful, and who forms in the world a new Israel, a spiritual community that is the forerunner, the often faint and flickering but nevertheless real foreshadowing, of the divine purpose for the well-being of the world.

TWO

The Growth of the Spirit Community

THE HARVEST: The Three Stages of the Kingdom

> The kingdom of God is as if someone would scatter seed on the ground, and would sleep and rise night and day, and the seed would sprout and grow, he does not know how. The earth produces of itself, first the stalk, then the head, then the full grain in the head. But when the grain is ripe, at once he goes in with his sickle, because the harvest has come.
>
> —Mark 4:26–29

THE SECOND PARABLE IN Mark's Gospel likens the kingdom of God to grain growing from a seed. What appears to be a different version of this parable is in Matthew's Gospel.[1] In the parable, the kingdom is not some future state where everything is perfect, and not a future Israel living wholly by Torah. It is something that grows and develops over time. But there will be a harvest, when the wheat is fully grown. Perhaps one might say that the full growth, that which grows to fulfilment in time, will be taken into the eternal being of God.

This is in some ways a traditional interpretation of the parable, though it introduces a theme of the final uniting of all things "in Christ," which may be new to many. C. H. Dodd, however, proposed that it was unlikely that Jesus was thinking about a future community of the Spirit at all, as something

1. Matt 13:24–30.

that would grow after his death.[2] Rather, Professor Dodd thought that the original point of the parable would have been to emphasize not a gradual growing but a present harvesting of the wheat. In his interpretation, the growth had already taken place, in the prophets of Israel and Judah, and the time of harvest had come. Now the disciples would have the task of reaping. They were to confront their hearers with a moment of decision for God, and this decision was of huge significance for them.

Dodd accepts that, especially in Matthew's version, there is reference to a coming final judgment. But this, he proposes, is a later addition by early Christians. For Jesus, he thinks, the judgment took place as people accepted or rejected the gospel. Dodd proposes a "realized eschatology," for which the kingdom had fully come in the person of Jesus, and there was to be no further "return in glory" after some delay. Thus, Jesus' teaching of the kingdom does not refer to something still to happen in the future, whether that was to be very soon or greatly delayed.

There is, I think, an important truth in Dodd's interpretation. The kingdom had, indeed, come in the person of Jesus, and in Dodd's words, "history had become the vehicle of the eternal."[3] Moreover, early Christians were mistaken if they thought that there would be a further coming of Christ in glory very soon in human history. They were certainly wrong in thinking it would happen within a generation, and as the centuries pass, it is increasingly unlikely that it will ever happen in a literal form. Nevertheless, unlike Professor Dodd, I think the disciples were not wrong in thinking that the kingdom had not fully come in the life of the Jesus community.

Professor Dodd proposes that the mystery of the kingdom is revealed precisely in the suffering and death of Jesus, and in the persecution of his disciples. "God's opposition to evil is shown in the suffering of its worst assaults."[4] This seems to me unduly paradoxical. There could hardly be said to have been any real judgment on evil, when evil continued apace in the world and even in the church. And as Dodd says, "Our destiny lies in the eternal order,"[5] and though this may be found to be true in the present to an important extent, the eternal order is not to be found very fully in any present moments of human history.

2. Dodd, *Parables of the Kingdom*, 131–38.

3. Dodd, *Parables of the Kingdom*, 147.

4. Dodd, *Parables of the Kingdom*, 61.

5. Dodd, *Parables of the Kingdom*, 156.

I resonate fully with Professor Dodd's emphasis that the kingdom had come and was present in Jesus. But Jesus after all called disciples and sent them out to proclaim the good news of the kingdom. He did not send them out just to proclaim the arrival of a terrible crisis in which they would all suffer. The parables do speak of a judgment on evil that would be expressed in the death of Jesus and in the destruction of the Jerusalem Temple. But that is not the proclamation of the new life of the kingdom. It is pointing out what the rejection of that proclamation would lead to, on the historical plane. It is important to remember that the gospel was meant to be good news of healing and reconciliation. Suffering and destruction might follow from rejection of the kingdom, but that was not the point of preaching. There has admittedly throughout the history of the churches been a tendency to revel in what they imagined as the horrors of the damned. But that tendency should be resisted, in view of the fact that the gospel says that God's love, even or especially for those who have rejected God, is unlimited even by death and hell.[6] More of that hereafter.

Professor Dodd insists that "the sacrificial death and resurrection of Christ . . . is, on the historical plane, the triumph of the cause of God, the coming of the Son of Man."[7] There is nothing more to expect within human history. Here "the absolute . . . has entered into time and space" and revealed its true character. Nevertheless, "the 'Day of the Son of Man' stands for the timeless fact,"[8] for an eternal order that the human mind cannot directly apprehend. Professor Dodd does think there is more to the story than historical events. Such events reflect eternal truths about death and resurrection.

In this I believe he is right. But I would want to say that these truths are not eternal in the sense of being timeless and unchanging. They refer to future realities in which living humans can participate. That participation may take two main forms. It may be a continuous growth towards a more perfect knowledge and love of God and God's creation. Or it may be a time of corrective punishment and purification in which repentance is still possible as people learn to confront their failures and the consequences of their harmful actions. These truths refer, in other words, to life in the age (the world) to come.

6. See Romans 8:38 and 39: "I am convinced that neither death . . . nor anything else in all creation, will be able to separate us from the love of God in Christ Jesus our Lord."

7. Dodd, *Parables of the Kingdom*, 81.

8. Dodd, *Parables of the Kingdom*, 82.

Beyond the first stage of the kingdom, when people are called to form a new society of the Spirit of Christ, there is a time of growth or purification in the world to come. Beyond that there is what is referred to in the Bible as the "universal restoration" (*apokatastasis*) of the created universe,[9] when there will be a "new heaven and a new earth," and the universe will be restored as a true and unrestricted sacrament of the glory of God. This stage is prefigured in what may be called a second stage of the kingdom, the existence of paradise, the "great feast" where Abraham and the prophets sit with those gathered from the whole world in the presence of God. This is perhaps best seen as the highest level of the world to come, in contrast to the lowest level, which is the "fire" of Gehenna or hades. It is not yet the third stage, the restoration of all things. It is to that third stage of the restored universe that Christ, the Son of Man, comes in glory. It may turn out that existence in such a world is the true destiny of those beings that have originated in this world of space and time, and matured in the afterlife worlds of purification and sanctification (which the church later came to refer to, in perhaps a rather unduly limited sense, as purgatory and paradise). When the redeeming work of God is completed, there will be a "restoration" of this world, this universe, in which all evil is finally destroyed, and all good retained and increased.

All this is so far beyond the conceptions of human minds, at the time of Jesus and even now, that it can only be spoken of in symbol and imagery. I am therefore obviously not claiming to give secret details of exactly what it is like. I am only pointing out that a condition of the ultimate triumph of God's love in a fallen world must presuppose something like this. The rule of Spirit begins in a new way with Jesus, and it will be completed in the eternal Word, which is incarnate in Jesus, and openly unveiled in the glorified form of the Son of Man. It is future-oriented, and promises a fulfilment of present created existence. It is not eternal in the sense of being timeless. It is a real future for real creatures, and the decisive move towards it begins with our response to the incarnate Word.

Jesus was, by calling disciples to give up all and follow him, founding a new sort of society of those who responded to the message. It would be an entirely reasonable hope that this society would grow from its small beginnings in Galilee. And, though Jesus' mission was to the Jews, the hope was surely that in time it would be extended to the gentiles, and this new society would be a people who would be a blessing to the world and a light to the

9. Acts 3:21.

nations. This would take time, and so the image of growth is a very suitable image of the kingdom.

The disciples were to call people into the kingdom, as if they were reaping a harvest ripe for the picking.[10] But it is a strange thought that such a calling, and the immediate response to it, was to be the end of the story. Disciples were to pray, "Your kingdom come, in earth as in heaven." While the new community would be, as Dodd puts it, a vehicle of the eternal, it would still be a very imperfect, fragmentary vehicle. It seems like the beginning of a long journey towards the eternal order, the full realization of the rule of God. Perhaps Dodd is right to be skeptical of evolutionary views that history will move towards a future perfection, and also of the view that there will be an immanent catastrophic event of divine intervention. But is he right to think that the kingdom came with Jesus, and though it continues to come to us in much the same way, things will never actually get any better?

The early theologians of Alexandria spoke of the eternal entering into time in Jesus, in order that we should enter into eternity. This double movement is, I think, central to Christian faith. Jesus puts eternity into human hearts in a new and definitive way. But that is in order that human hearts shall be united to the eternal, and that is not something that happens in history, whether soon or late. It is something that happens in a spiritual realm, to which this life is a preparation and proving ground.

Thus, this parable of the growth and harvesting of wheat is not merely saying, as Dodd and Jeremias seem to suggest, that the disciples are to invite all, both bad and good, into the kingdom. It was, even in the mouth of Jesus, saying that a new community of the Spirit would grow and flourish, and become a community for the whole world. When the community is full grown, there will be a harvest. The inner meaning is that the community and its members will develop through various stages, until they are ready to be received into God. The community is the place where the Spirit grows within human lives, and prepares them for life in the world to come, which is the uniting of all things in Christ. There is from the first what has been called an eschatological dimension to the parable. That is to say, the parable points to a belief about the ultimate goal of the whole cosmos. One does not have to think of this as a later addition by the early church.

10. Luke 10:2.

WHEAT AND TARES, THE NET: The Idea of Hell

> He put before them another parable: "The kingdom of heaven may be compared to someone who sowed good seed in his field; but while everybody was asleep, an enemy came and sowed weeds among the wheat, and then went away. So when the plants came up and bore grain, then the weeds appeared as well. And the slaves of the householder came and said to him, 'Master, did you not sow good seed in your field? Where, then, did these weeds come from?' He answered, 'An enemy has done this.' The slaves said to him, 'Then do you want us to go and gather them?' But he replied, 'No; for in gathering the weeds you would uproot the wheat along with them. Let both of them grow together until the harvest; and at harvest time I will tell the reapers, Collect the weeds first and bind them in bundles to be burned, but gather the wheat into my barn.'" . . .
>
> Then he left the crowds and went into the house. And his disciples approached him, saying, "Explain to us the parable of the weeds of the field." He answered, "The one who sows the good seed is the Son of Man; the field is the world, and the good seed are the children of the kingdom; the weeds are the children of the evil one, and the enemy who sowed them is the devil; the harvest is the end of the age, and the reapers are angels. Just as the weeds are collected and burned up with fire, so will it be at the end of the age. The Son of Man will send his angels, and they will collect out of his kingdom all causes of sin and all evildoers, and they will throw them into the furnace of fire, where there will be weeping and gnashing of teeth. Then the righteous will shine like the sun in the kingdom of their Father. Let anyone with ears listen!"
>
> —Matthew 13:24–30, 36–43

When Matthew relates this parable of the growing wheat, however, he introduces a new consideration. Tares grow alongside the wheat.[11] The kingdom, the growing community of the Spirit, is not free from evil. It is in fact an ambiguous community, where good and bad are mixed, not a pure community of the holy.

Matthew, like Mark, speaks of a final harvest. But Matthew, who typically stresses the negative throughout his gospel, adds the element

11. Matt 13:25.

of judgment where the wheat is gathered into a barn, and the weeds are burned in a fiery furnace, "where there will be weeping and gnashing of teeth."[12]

We have to take account of these very horrifying images of being burned in a fiery furnace or of being cast into outer darkness. Matthew uses such expressions in five parables, and they have helped to give rise to the widespread Christian idea of hell as a place of torture from which there is no escape. Even Professor Jeremias says that the frequency of such frightening images is "alarming," and they certainly cast doubt on the idea that God is a being of unlimited and universal love. Yet it is in Matthew's Gospel that the Sermon on the Mount[13] clearly puts into the mouth of Jesus the teaching that it is good to love one's enemies, that one should never be angry, and even that one should not resist evil. If that is good, and if our goodness is to be an imitation of God's perfection (Matt 5:48), how could God possibly throw people into a fiery furnace?

The image of a burning fiery furnace occurs most obviously in the book of Daniel, and the story of three Jews who were thrown into the furnace, but emerged unharmed, because God delivered them.[14] Matthew's victims are not said to be delivered, but they do weep and gnash their teeth, so they are obviously not burned to ashes, as they would be if it was a real furnace. Gnashing or grinding your teeth together is a sign of frustration, remorse, or anger. Combined with weeping, it undoubtedly points to a state of sorrow and despair. It is the mental state that is important, not some miraculous existence in the middle of a furnace. This prompts two main thoughts: that this is using a well-known biblical physical image for a time of spiritual testing, and that God can deliver people even when they are in such a furnace. The fact that Matthew can also use images of a prison and of outer darkness for the fate of the unjust strongly suggests that these are all symbols for some future spiritual state which will be highly unpleasant, and will be the result of what people have done before they died.

What seems to be implied is that those who have rejected the commands of love will after death experience states of mental anguish, presumably with a recognition that they have brought misery on themselves as well as on others by their conduct during life. This is not torture by someone else, but self-torture at seeing and experiencing the terrible consequences

12. Matt 13:42.

13. Matt 5–7.

14. Dan 3:15–20.

of unjust action, without the possibility of ignoring such consequences any longer. While it sounds wicked to throw people into a furnace, however bad they are, it is not wicked to compel criminals to face up to the harm and pain they have caused, and to see how their actions are truly destroying any possibility of their own happiness and fulfilment. It is important, therefore, to reject any literal interpretation of these sayings, but to take them as exaggerated and, precisely for that reason, memorable images of what your unjust actions will result in for yourself, when all pretences and self-justifications are swept away, and you at last see yourself for what you have made yourself during life.

Dominic Crossan thinks these admittedly violent images are so bad that Matthew must have made them up himself, and Jesus, correctly reported in the Sermon on the Mount, could not possibly have used them. However, the Gospels record many highly exaggerated images used by Jesus—like a camel going through the eye of a needle, or pulling out and throwing away an eye—and I see no reason why he might not have used such images to make the point very forcibly that injustice is a form of turning away from God that will lead to self-blame and self-hatred. This state of consciousness is like burning in a fire of recrimination, or like being in the darkness of losing all possibility of loving companionship. My claim is only true, however, if the time of teeth-gnashing does not go on forever. God's goodness, which is the heart of Jesus' teaching, always cares for those who are lost, and is able, and always wishes, to draw them from the flames if and when they come to trust in God.

I think that it is very important always to bear in mind that God is love,[15] and that God's love is unending. Maybe Matthew had not quite got this message. Certainly, his words have generated a widespread belief among Christians that there is a "hell" from which there is no escape. The terrible consequences of this belief have included burning infidels at the stake and have been used to justify inflicting horrifying tortures on those who are anyway thought to be destined for eternal torture in hell. Christians need to identify the roots of these wicked beliefs in the New Testament itself, and to counteract them with a firm insistence that no one is ever beyond the hope of redemption by God. That is, after all, what the "good news" of the kingdom is.

The kingdom is not finally gained until all evil is eliminated. It follows that for most Christians there must be a time of purification, which will

15. 1 John 4:8, 16.

bring them to a state that will guard them for ever from the temptations of evil. For many, that time will involve the recognition of and remorse for what they have been. It will involve tears and even agony of mind. Nevertheless, it should not be forgotten that parables are *not literal descriptions* of what will happen in future.

In Matthew's interpretation of the Parable of the Wheat and the Tares,[16] the righteous or just (*dikaioi*) will be gathered into a barn, or shine like the sun. That is not a literal description (people could hardly shine like the sun and be in a barn at the same time. Anyway, they would probably not like being in a barn very much either), though it suggests that the righteous will be happy and fulfilled. Similarly, the fiery furnace is not a literal description. The suggestion, however, is clearly that the unrighteous will not enter into the presence of God, and will be unhappy and regretful. The parable does not say how long they will endure the "flames," or whether they can ever escape. The first letter to the Corinthians holds that "the fire will test what sort of work each has done," and "if the work is burned . . . the builder will be saved, but only as through fire."[17] The book of Jude recommends that Christians "save others by snatching them out of the fire."[18] So it is not clear that for Matthew there is talk of unending pain, from which there is no possibility of escape. The key teaching is clear, however, that there will be a judgment, when the unjust will be separated from God, and the righteous will be with God.

The Parable of the Net repeats this theme of a division between the evil (bad fish who are thrown away) and the just.

> Again, the kingdom of heaven is like a net that was thrown into the sea and caught fish of every kind; when it was full, they drew it ashore, sat down, and put the good into baskets but threw out the bad. So it will be at the end of the age. The angels will come out and separate the evil from the righteous and throw them into the furnace of fire, where there will be weeping and gnashing of teeth.
>
> —Matthew 13:47–50

It is noteworthy that in both parables the division is not between the faithful and the unfaithful, but between the just and the unjust. This division is emphasized in Matthew's picture (not usually classified as a parable)

16. Matt 13:36–43.
17. 1 Cor 3:13–15.
18. Jude 23.

of the Last Judgment, where people are divided into sheep and goats. The sheep (the just) are those who feed the hungry, welcome strangers, clothe the naked, and visit the sick and those in prison. The goats (the unjust) are sent off to "age-long" fire for punishment.[19] There is no mention of faith or belief in Jesus here. But there is, uniquely in the Gospels, a phrase that is often translated as "eternal punishment" (*kolasin aionion*). This phrase is one main source of the belief that there is unending punishment in hell—though it is not so often noticed that such punishment is not for unbelievers, but for the unjust, whatever they believe.

Furthermore, this translation is unfortunate. There is a punishment, but both the words *kolasin* and *aionion* are notoriously hard to translate. In Greek, *kolasin* can mean "correction" or "corrective punishment." It does not entail torture or retributive punishment for the sake of it, whatever the outcome. Punishment exists for the sake of reform or correction, which implies that correction is possible, and may even, given enough time and patience, succeed for everyone. As for the word *aionion*, it means literally "for an age" or "of the age." It does not mean literally "everlasting," as the King James version of the English Bible has it. We do not know how long an "age" is, but in general an age would have an end (like "the age of Enlightenment," for example). Therefore, the phrase *kolasin aionion* could quite properly and much more helpfully be translated as "corrective punishment for an indeterminate length of time" or simply as "the punishment of the age to come" (without any comment on its duration).

The crucial contrast is between "eternal death" and "eternal life." If eternal life means life with the eternal God,[20] then eternal death means existence without God. In other words, "eternal" can refer more to a *quality of being* than to a temporal quantity. Of course, one hopes that life with God will last for ever, since God endures for and even beyond all ages, and the Christian promise is that it will.[21] But it would be absurd to hope that life without God will last for ever. Anyone who is merciful, including God, would hope that life without God, though it may last for an age, or for some ages, would eventually come to an end, whether by final extinction or by repentance and reconciliation to God.

19. Matt 25:31–36.

20. John 17:3.

21. 1 Cor 15:42–44.

GOD AND GOODNESS

The parables do not resolve these hard questions about the fate of the unjust. They just stress that in this life the just and unjust are mixed up together, that the just need to develop and grow, and that at the end of "the age" the just will live with God and the unjust will (in Matthew) receive a punishment suited to their evil doing. As I suggested in my comments on the Parable of the Harvest, there seem to be two stages in the coming of God's kingdom before the final third stage, the "restoration" of all things. The first stage is one of growing in the Spirit, in a world that has fallen into evil. That evil will affect even the community of the Spirit. The second stage is after death, when some will continue to grow in the knowledge and love of goodness, and others will need to pass through a time of learning true sorrow, repentance, and their need for the redeeming love of God.

A question that is left unaddressed is what happens to the just who strive for goodness, but who do not become disciples of Jesus, or who are good but not religious. It is clear that religion alone is not enough, for the growing kingdom contains tares as well as wheat. "Faith by itself, if it has no works, is dead."[22] As Jesus says elsewhere, many who expect to be members of the kingdom, including many pious Jews (and Christians) will find themselves excluded.[23] The picture of the Last Judgement, in Matthew 25, strongly suggests that *all* humans ("all the nations," v. 32) will be judged, not on what they believe, but on whether or not they have been just and merciful.

Why, then, if this is true, should anyone believe in God? The obvious reason is simply that it is true that there is a God. People can be good without belief in God. But Jesus' parables teach that the knowledge and love of God adds something very important to human attempts to be just and compassionate. Jesus teaches that God approaches us—"the rule of God has come near"[24]—and offers to plant the seed of divine love within us. This seed grows within us, and with our cooperation it brings to us the fruits of joy and peace, and to the world through us the fruits of kindness and generosity. When the end of all ages comes, love alone will remain, evil will be banished, and love, fully united with its source in the unlimited love of God, will endure for ever. The difference God makes is threefold: (a)

22. Jas 2:17.

23. Matt 8:11 and 12.

24. Mark 1:15.

that God plants the divine love within us, a love that is infinitely stronger than our own; (b) God ensures that goodness will ultimately triumph over evil; and (c) God promises that we can personally share in that triumph. These beliefs, if they are sincere, will transform the moral life from one of obedience to stern duty into a life of loving union with a reality of supreme goodness that draws us ever closer to itself. That is a significant difference.

Many people today think that we do not need God to seek delight in beautiful things, intelligent understanding of the world, and compassionate action for the sake of others. They even think that a God would make such seeking harder, because God would demand obedience to an arbitrary set of commands, enforced by fear of punishment, whether or not those commands make for human welfare. Perhaps, they think, if we seek to obey God, we should renounce all earthly pleasures, including pleasure in beauty. Perhaps we should be content just to worship God with hymns and prayers, and not seek for truths that may turn out to undermine faith. Perhaps concern for God's truth might lead us to shun or even hate unbelievers and those who deny God. Perhaps morality should be separated from belief in God altogether.

Jesus' teachings should be sufficient to reject all those suppositions. Jesus insisted that we should care for the poor, and love even our enemies. He was reputed to be a winebibber, not a great ascetic, and he certainly enjoyed many feasts, and even spoke of heaven itself as a great feast. He stood in the Jewish tradition that the world was created good, and was to be enjoyed as such. And he came to give the gift of joy to his disciples, even though they apparently moaned and quarrelled a lot. Jesus stood for the value of human existence, the enjoyment of God's creation, and for more abundant life. There was nothing he was more opposed to than obedience to religious rules for their own sake, without consideration for the well-being of others.

Discipleship of Jesus is life-affirming, not life-denying. Nevertheless, can one not affirm life without God? The answer to this question should be an unequivocal yes! The good do not have to be religious, and the religious do not have to be good. Yet there is a deep connection between goodness and God. If there is a God of supreme goodness, then goodness is rooted in the ultimate nature of reality. If you ask what is ultimately real, and you say that the ultimately real is supreme goodness, and you really believe it, this will affect your view of the world in a very fundamental way.

The most important effect will be that you believe that at the heart of reality there exists a supremely beautiful and desirable reality. It exerts an attraction on you just by being what it is. Just as a beautiful landscape or piece of music may attract you, so an apprehension of God will attract you just because of God's intrinsic worthwhileness. This is one important part of "worship." Worship is not telling God how great you think God is. It is experiencing great happiness in the apprehension of supreme beauty.

If, in addition, this being has a purpose of enabling you to share in its nature, of sharing its own happiness and perfection, it will naturally evoke a sense of gratefulness and devotion. Realizing that your whole existence, and your belief in an overwhelmingly good future, depends on God, and that God wills the best for you, the most natural reaction is one of love and trust. It is not that some very powerful being issues commands of any sort it wants, and forces you to obey them. It is rather that the existence of a supreme beauty, wisdom, and happiness will attract you to union with itself. If it issues demands, these will be pointers on the way to obtain that supreme purpose, which will fulfil your life. We will follow these demands, if we are wise, not out of fear, but because they show the way to the greatest worthwhile happiness that we could achieve.

It is true, and Christian believers should accept it gladly, that many people feel the demands of moral obligation, and can be morally heroic, whether or not they believe in God. In a rather similar way, artists and musicians can be great, yet not believe in God. So, obviously, can the greatest scientists and mathematicians. Sometimes the non-religious can achieve more than the religious. Verdi, for instance, wrote a truly great requiem Mass, but was not a believer.

There is, however, more to be said about this. Many great artists and scientists feel that there is some transcendent dimension that enables them to produce the work they do, something that has been symbolized by speaking of the Muses who inspire great works. In the case of morality, there is the feeling that there is something normative, something demanding, about the obligation to help others. It is as if something more than just personal satisfaction is present, some task that one feels "called" to undertake, or, in the arts, some work that just seems to shape itself as one is taken over by a greater force. It may be said that this is not "religious," because it does not involve commitment to all sorts of complicated dogmas, or to some grand but rather authoritarian institution. Nevertheless, in morality, as in art and science, there are many pointers to transcendence, to powers that seem to work in and through the human mind. For the Christian, these are pointers to the creative Spirit of God, and they certainly hint at active powers beyond the physical and the everyday.

It is also the case that when morality, art, and science lose touch with any sense that there is some sort of objective, more-than-merely-human dimension that demands attention to what have been called the "transcendental values" of truth, beauty, and goodness, then morality can come to be seen as just some sort of obsolete remnant of primitive tribal taboos, art can be seen as just a vehicle for sexual pleasure or entertainment, and science can be seen as a means to increasing control over nature and obtaining wealth.

This, I think, is because it is hard for an atheist to find a fully intelligible place for moral demands—which call for sacrifice for the sake of others—in a universe that is at bottom morally neutral, without purpose or value, and indifferent to moral concerns. Such demands tend to be seen as voluntary choices, ways in which some people choose to live. Most of us admire them for helping those in need, and perhaps it is sufficient reason for choosing to do so that they feel pity for those who are less fortunate than themselves. They choose to love, without hope of reward or even of success, and the fundamental choice to love is a basic motivation that all believers in God must admire.

This is, in fact, the fundamental choice that faces all Christians too. Some Christians choose love, and some do not. It would be silly to say that Christians are morally better than atheists. Yet there is a difference between Christians and atheists. If Christians choose love, it is because they believe they are loved by one who is supremely beautiful and good, and thus supremely attractive, because they believe this being wants them to fulfil the purpose of creating goodness in the world, and because they believe that this purpose will ultimately be achieved, so that no loving action will be useless or in vain.

For Christians, there is not a huge and almost inexplicable gap between the moral indifference of the universe and an absolute commitment to justice and compassion. Having such a commitment will be carrying out the purpose that is inherent in the creation of this universe. The demands of morality are not just principles they decide to observe, for no reason other than that they just seem right. Moral demands are built into the universe itself. For the universe does not consist of nothing but physical particles obeying purposeless and unconscious laws of nature. The universe depends upon a conscious being of supreme value and moral purpose. The laws of morality are an essential part of the being of God. They are the things that humans ought to do because this is their purpose and proper function. That purpose is that many forms of goodness (states and processes of intrinsic value) should be created and contemplated, and the Creator promises that such goodness will never be lost, but will remain in the divine mind for ever.

Is there value and purpose in the universe? Is there a great wisdom that calls us to pursue this purpose and promises that this value will be realized? Atheists are bound to say "no," and in saying that they give their moral choices, however heroic they are, no supporting justification. Indeed, they have to say that moral commitment needs no justification. It is just obvious that one ought to do what is right. But if someone says that is not obvious, and that moral commitment is little more than social convention or an obsolete leftover from some primitive or childhood survival-mechanism, there is not much the atheist can say.

If, however, there really is a God, a supreme good in which humans—and perhaps all personal beings in the universe—can share, then there is a justification for moral commitment, namely, that there is a purpose of great value that can be achieved by such commitment, that there is a being who will ensure that this purpose will be realized, and that an overwhelmingly strong reason for pursuing this purpose is that it is the purpose of a being of supreme value, knowledge of whom is supremely worthwhile, and relationship with whom will bring all sentient beings to their proper fulfilment.

Is this appeal to ultimate personal well-being selfish? No, because our attention will be focussed not primarily on ourselves and our own pleasure, but on the object of our desire, and because God's purpose is that all sentient beings, not just humans, should obtain fulfilment. Indeed, it is not possible to achieve fulfilment without positive cooperation with other beings, and sharing with them what we desire for ourselves. Such sharing in creating and savoring new forms of goodness is itself one of the greatest goods. It is when the self is taken out of itself in contemplating something supremely good and sharing with others in creatively seeking new forms of goodness that it achieves its greatest degree of fulfilment.

Goodness can certainly exist without religious belief, and morality can exist without religion. As Jesus constantly pointed out, religion can be a primary source of hypocrisy, vindictive hatred of others, and feelings of moral superiority. Yet Christians believe in a God of supreme wisdom and love, who wills fulfilment and happiness for all beings who are capable of it, whose rule over humans is the presence of divine wisdom and love in human hearts, and whose purpose is that all creation will be fulfilled in the life of God. This belief, if true, provides an overwhelming reason for obeying the supreme commands of God, which are: love of neighbor, which really means love for all sentient beings, and love of God, which means love of all the many forms of beauty and goodness in the world, because they are created and loved by God, and also love of the one who created them.

The kingdom or rule of God therefore includes all possible forms of goodness. It is not an alternative to the ordinary pleasures we find in life; it includes them. We should give up our desires only insofar as they are disordered and self-serving. We should renounce the desire to possess things for ourselves, to the exclusion of others. We should renounce undue attachment even to beauty and knowledge if they make us slaves to ambition and pride. But we should renounce such desires only to realize a nobler and less self-centred desire, the desire to know God, who includes all goods in Godself and who will ensure that a society of realized goodness will come to exist and will endure for ever. To work for that end is to "seek the kingdom of heaven." It will in this world require a degree of self-renunciation. Yet even now we can experience a foreshadowing of that supreme good towards which the creation moves, drawn by the divine love that moves the stars and the hearts of men and women.

It is in this sense that Jesus, expressing the best of Jewish tradition, teaches that justice springs from a genuine love for others, that love of others is evoked by the recognition that they are loved by God, and that we naturally desire to love what God loves. We experience the love of God for us, and our love is the expression of a response to the supreme beauty and overflowing goodness of God: "we love because He first loved us."[25] What we, and what all people, fail to show of love, God is ready to forgive. What we cannot do of ourselves, God will do in and through us. God, who is supreme mercy, will forgive and unite to the divine life all who turn to him, whether now or at some later time.[26]

Peter said in his sermon at Caesarea, "In every nation anyone who fears Him [God] and does what is right is acceptable to Him."[27] Those who give their lives for the sake of justice are acceptable to God, and that is what the picture of the Last Judgement implies. But they too stand in need of forgiveness for many things, their commitment to duty would be enriched by a knowledge of that perfect beauty and goodness which is God, and their

25. 1 John 4:19.

26. "God our Saviour desires everyone to be saved": 1 Tim 2:4. What God desires, God will make possible.

27. Acts 10:34.

commitment to goodness will be validated by the fulfilment of all things in the divine perfection.

The Spirit has drawn near to all, though, like the just who stand before the judgment throne of God in Matthew's picture, they may not yet know it for what it truly is. One major task of the community of the Spirit is to make this known, by actions as well as by words.

MUSTARD-SEED AND YEAST: A New Covenant with God

> He also said, "With what can we compare the kingdom of God, or what parable will we use for it? It is like a mustard seed, which, when sown upon the ground, is the smallest of all the seeds on earth; yet when it is sown it grows up and becomes the greatest of all shrubs, and puts forth large branches, so that the birds of the air can make nests in its shade."
>
> —Mark 4:30–32

Jesus compares the kingdom of God to a tiny mustard seed that grows to become a great shrub. Matthew and Luke add to Mark's account a short parable about a woman who hid leaven in three measures of flour, until it was all leavened.[28]

> He told them another parable: "The kingdom of heaven is like yeast that a woman took and mixed in with three measures of flour until all of it was leavened."
>
> —Matthew 13:33

Both these very short parables pose intriguing problems of interpretation. The Parable of the Mustard Seed in Mark correctly says that mustard seeds grow up to be shrubs, and that birds might make nests in their shade. But Matthew and Luke turn the shrub (which is not really very large) into a huge tree, in the branches of which the birds make their nests. Commentators have been very upset about this difference, but I cannot see a major problem. This is, after all, a parable, a fiction, not a botanical lecture, so why can this not be just a bit of magic realism, for which bushes turning into trees is only to be expected? Although it is undeniable that not all the precise terms in the various Gospels can be original with Jesus, because they are different from each other, the main point is clear, that from tiny beginnings great

28. Matt 13:33.

consequences can follow. Dominic Crossan says bluntly that the Parable of the Mustard Seed should not be called a parable of growth.[29] It is a "contrast parable," which contrasts the smallness of human effort with the greatness of God's gift. In this, he follows C. H. Dodd and Joachim Jeremias, who think that any growth was in the past, and the parable was concerned with the miraculous presence of the kingdom of God.

The trouble with this view is that the present kingdom, when Jesus spoke, was very small indeed. It may have been present, but it was hardly even a large shrub. It does look as though, since the present kingdom is so very small (maybe only in the person of Jesus), the emphasis must be upon growth, and the image suggests that such growth will be spread out over time. The implication is that Jesus' message of the kingdom starts with just a few disciples, but is destined to grow into a great movement. Whether he thinks of this as happening within Judaism or as reaching out to the whole world is unclear. Given that many gentiles had already entered the church by the time this Gospel was written, in its context in Mark it must be seen as applying to the whole world, even though Jesus was concerned in his ministry with the Jewish people.

We have seen that this phase of the kingdom does not just apply to a group of holy people, but includes both the good and the imperfect. Robert Funk holds that the one-sentence Parable of the Yeast contains three significant features.[30] First, "yeast" is always in Jewish thought a symbol of evil or impurity; so perhaps it stands here for the acceptance that the kingdom will contain the outcasts of society, not just the religiously pious. It could also, in my view, make yeast stand for the gentiles, who could be considered ritually impure from a Jewish point of view, and who were becoming the dominant element in the new churches. Crossan notes this point too, that yeast was always regarded as unclean or impure in Jewish thought. He suggests that the point of this parable was to break down or question the clean/unclean distinction, and thus emphasize the solidarity of all humans and query the conventional barriers between different sorts of people. On the other hand, the parable stresses the huge amount of bread that is produced, and so it seems at least as concerned with the growth of the kingdom as with breaking down social conventions.

Second, the yeast was "hidden," which implies that the kingdom works invisibly within the world, not as an overt power but as an often

29. Crossan, *Power of Parable*, 50

30. Funk, *Jesus as Precursor*, on "The Parable of the Leaven."

unnoticed influence. And third, Funk says that the "three measures of flour"—an improbably large amount—is a reminder of descriptions of Old Testament sacrifices to God, which often speak of offering three measures of some substance. It is thus suggestive of the fact that the kingdom calls for a sacrificial offering of life to God in the service of others. It may be thought that this analysis pushes allegory too far; it does completely contradict any claim that parables are not allegories. But the analysis is thought-provoking and intriguing. It is a good example of the way in which parables are polysemic, and can be expansively elaborated in ways that may well be spiritually illuminating.

In a way, it helps to explain the nature of God's covenant with, first the Jews, and secondly, the disciples of Jesus. Such a covenant is a calling to sacrificial service, not to political or religious dominance, and it is not the selection of a few holy people to have an exclusive relationship to God.

There has always been a problem within Judaism of why the Jews were chosen to be brought into a covenant with God, and of what this means for the rest of the world. The problem became even greater for the first Christ-followers, for they had to decide whether the gentiles who became disciples of Jesus needed to convert to Judaism and become Torah-obedient, and they had to explain why they, so few out of the mass of humanity, had been called into what they saw as a new covenant with God through Jesus.

The negative interpretation, that only Christians would inherit eternal life while all others would be excluded, seems hugely uncharitable and unmerciful, and is incompatible with any perception of God as compassionate and merciful. This negative interpretation of covenant has rarely been held by Jews, who do not condemn gentiles to hell for not being Jews, but for whom the Torah is given in part to separate them off from gentiles as having a special form of commitment (sometimes conceived as a "marriage," as in Jeremiah), initiated by God.[31]

If one person marries another, that does not mean that they are indifferent to other people. On the contrary, a good marriage is one that is hospitable and kind to others, and extends the mutual love of those who are lucky enough to know mutual love, to embrace loving service to a wider community.

If the Jewish people are bound to God in mutual love, they are meant to extend that love in appropriate ways to all people. Moreover, it does not follow from the fact that God "marries" Israel to Godself that God does

31. Jer 31:32.

not care about or relate in other ways to other people. Jews are bound by love to the God of Abraham and Isaac. But that same God is also the God of Indians and Chinese, Europeans and Africans, and because God is love, God will care for their good as much as for the good of the Israelites. In this regard, consider the astonishing oracle in Isaiah 19, in which God says the following about two of Israel's greatest enemies—Egypt and Assyria:

> On that day there will be five cities in the land of Egypt that speak the language of Canaan and swear allegiance to the LORD of hosts. One of these will be called the City of the Sun.
>
> On that day there will be an altar to the LORD in the center of the land of Egypt, and a pillar to the LORD at its border. It will be a sign and a witness to the LORD of hosts in the land of Egypt; when they cry to the LORD because of oppressors, he will send them a savior, and will defend and deliver them. The LORD will make himself known to the Egyptians; and the Egyptians will know the LORD on that day, and will worship with sacrifice and burnt offering, and they will make vows to the LORD and perform them. The LORD will strike Egypt, striking and healing; they will return to the LORD, and he will listen to their supplications and heal them.
>
> On that day there will be a highway from Egypt to Assyria, and the Assyrian will come into Egypt, and the Egyptian into Assyria, and the Egyptians will worship with the Assyrians.
>
> On that day Israel will be the third with Egypt and Assyria, a blessing in the midst of the earth, whom the LORD of hosts has blessed, saying, "Blessed be Egypt my people, and Assyria the work of my hands, and Israel my heritage."
>
> —Isaiah 19:18–25

In other words, the covenant between God and Israel is meant to be "a light to lighten the gentiles," an expression of how to be rightly related to God from which all people can learn, though gentiles will no doubt have their own ways of relating to the supreme spiritual basis of the world. The people of Israel, however, are called to be a medium through which the divine love can serve the needs of the wider world. The Jewish covenant is a calling to manifest what divine love is when it informs a human community, and to be a medium of that divine love in service to the world. Jews are not "chosen to be saved"—hardly a Jewish expression—though God did promise to liberate them from oppression by other peoples, so that they could be free to follow the way of life to which God had called them.

Jews were to be "the priests of the earth" ("You shall be for me a priestly kingdom"),[32] not a spiritually advanced elite.

The biblical story of the history of the Jews shows how the people called by God failed in many ways, how they were an ambiguous people who often turned away from God. The Bible relates how they suffered defeat and exile, but how a faithful remnant always remained, and looked forward to a time when they could be both free and faithful to the covenant in their own homeland.

Jesus inherited this story, and when he preached that "the kingdom had come near," he claimed that these ancient Jewish hopes were about to be fulfilled in a dramatically new way. Jesus himself embodied the "faithful remnant" in his own person; he suffered and died; and he inaugurated, his followers believe, a new covenant, prophesied by Jeremiah,[33] writing the law of love in people's hearts, giving them personal knowledge of the Lord, and forgiving their sins.

This new covenant did not rescind the old covenant. But it offered a new path of relating to God through the Spirit to those who could accept it, though the ancient covenant of full Torah observance will remain until the end of human history. And it extended that covenant to a new people, not just the children of Abraham and Isaac. This new people would also be priests of the earth, and their calling, like that of the Jews (and preferably in fellowship with observant Jews, though tragically this did not happen), would be to manifest the love of God by serving and transforming the world by love and compassion.

These parables, to my mind, suggest that Jesus looked for a new community that would grow throughout the world, which would never be free of ambiguity, but which would be a transforming influence in society, being a sign and expression of divine love and concern for the well-being of all, and a community in which such love would be proclaimed, confirmed, and cultivated. The first phase of the kingdom of God, it seems, is the church, in the sense of a fellowship of those who strive to live by the Spirit,[34] and share in the divine nature.[35] But it is vitally important not to identify the institution of the church (any church!) with those who are guaranteed eternal life, or with a political ruling class on the world stage. As Jesus said, "Whoever

32. Exod 19:6.

33. Jer 31:33–34.

34. Gal 5:16.

35. 2 Pet 1:4.

wishes to be first among you must be slave of all."[36] The task of the church is to mediate the salvation of God to the whole world, not to be the exclusive society of the few who are destined for salvation.

36. Mark 10:44.

THREE

The Universal Community of the Spirit

THE FIG TREE: The Prophets

THE THEME OF A new, universal covenant is continued in parables that warn of immanent judgment on Israel and upon her religious leaders. It is important to remember that proclamations of doom upon Israel were a frequent part of the Jewish prophetic repertoire. They are not a condemnation of Judaism itself, nor do they imply that God's covenant with Israel has been ended. Jesus is part of this Jewish prophetic tradition when he criticizes the religious leaders of Israel for their hypocrisy and self-righteous pride. He does announce a new covenant of the Spirit, and he does foresee the ending of the Jewish priesthood and of temple worship. But he was a faithful Jew, and called for the spiritual renewal of Judaism, not its ending.

Luke 13:6–9 tells of a man who planted a fig tree and, finding no fruit on it, decided to cut it down. But his vine dresser persuaded him to leave it for another year, and then decide whether to keep or destroy it.

> Then he told this parable: "A man had a fig tree planted in his vineyard; and he came looking for fruit on it and found none. So he said to the gardener, 'See here! For three years I have come looking for fruit on this fig tree, and still I find none. Cut it down! Why should it be wasting the soil?'He replied, 'Sir, let it alone for one more year, until I dig around it and put manure on it. If it bears fruit next year, well and good; but if not, you can cut it down.'"
>
> —Luke 13:6–9

This simple story clearly refers to Israel, and to the urgent need for her people to repent or face destruction. Jesus' ministry was urgent, and is wholly in line with that of the prophets of ancient Israel.

Another parable about a fig tree is found in all the Synoptic Gospels.

> Then he told them a parable: "Look at the fig tree and all the trees; as soon as they sprout leaves you can see for yourselves and know that summer is already near. So also, when you see these things taking place, you know that the kingdom of God is near. Truly I tell you, this generation will not pass away until all things have taken place. Heaven and earth will pass away, but my words will not pass away."
>
> —Luke 21:29–33

As people see the fig tree come into leaf, they know that summer is near. So his hearers should know that the kingdom of God is near (or, in Matthew and Mark, that "he" is at the very gates). They all add that "this generation will not pass away until all [these] things have taken place."

The prophets often warned of imminent doom upon Israel, and the need for moral reform, but also spoke of a hope for renewal and new life. This hope takes various forms, some more nationalistic and vindictive than others. Though the prophecies recorded in what Christians call the Old Testament were made in differing historical situations, they all have to deal with the fact that Judah and Israel, the only remnants of the twelve tribes, have continually been oppressed, occupied, and carried into exile. How could the people with whom God had made an eternal covenant suffer in this way? One common prophetic response is to foretell terrible and catastrophic judgments on the oppressors of the Jews.

Thus Micah writes, "O daughter Zion . . . you shall beat in pieces many people, and shall devote their gain to the LORD."[1] And Zechariah says, "the clans of Judah . . . shall devour to the right and to the left all the surrounding peoples."[2] Judah will have revenge on her enemies, and "strangers shall stand and feed your flocks, foreigners shall till you land and dress your vines."[3] All foreign oppressors will be destroyed, or will serve Israel and come to worship Israel's God.

1. Mic 4:13.
2. Zech 12:5 and 6.
3. Isa 61:5.

Sometimes this destruction is taken to the utmost extent: "I will utterly sweep away everything from the face of the earth, says the LORD. . . . I will cut off humanity from the face of the earth."[4] It sounds as if there will be nothing left. Even the animals, birds, and fish will be swept away. Isaiah goes even further: "All the host of heaven shall rot away, and the skies roll up like a scroll."[5] And Joel adds, "The sun and moon are darkened and the stars withdraw their shining."[6] It looks as if the whole universe will be destroyed.

It is obvious that matters have got very exaggerated. Zephaniah goes on to say, "Perhaps you may be hidden on the day of the LORD's wrath."[7] However, we need to understand that these descriptions of doom are hyperbolic, for we find that alongside them the same prophets will offer hope, even expansive hope. Thus, Zechariah says, "Many peoples and strong nations shall come to seek the LORD of hosts in Jerusalem."[8] There are some people left after all. And as we have seen, Isaiah (or one of the writers of this part of Isaiah) even has God blessing the two greatest enemies of Israel—Egypt and Assyria.[9] There will be a time of peace and blessing: "The LORD will comfort Zion . . . and will make her wilderness like Eden, her desert like the garden of the Lord; joy and gladness will be found in her."[10]

The prophets swing between saying that Israel will destroy all her enemies, that there is a remnant of Israel who will live in a renewed and fruitful Zion, and that all nations will come to serve Israel joyfully.

It may seem unfair to patch such prophetic passages together, as though they are all parts of one agreed message. My point, however, is precisely to show that there is no agreed message. What different prophets are saying is that evil will be confounded and peace and justice will come. But they have very different ideas about how and when this will happen.

It should also be said that the main prophetic message is to call the people of Judah to a renewed commitment to morality and obedience to God's purpose. "Is not this the fast that I choose: to loose the bonds of injustice, to undo the thongs of the yoke, to let the oppressed go free, . . . to

4. Zeph 1:3.
5. Isa 34:4.
6. Joel 2:10.
7. Zeph 2:3.
8. Zech 8:22.
9. Isa 19:25.
10. Isa 51:3.

share your bread with the hungry, and bring the homeless poor into your house?"[11] Some prophets even criticize the sacrificial temple rites: "I hate, I despise your festivals, . . . even though you offer me your burnt offerings and grain-offerings, I will not accept them, . . . but let justice roll down like waters, and righteousness like an ever-flowing stream."[12] Moral renewal was the main concern of the prophets.

This is the background to the New Testament passages that some have taken to be about the end of the world. The first thing to say is that *they are not all literally true*, and indeed that they do not all say one consistent thing. There is huge exaggeration and use of poetic imagery. The second thing is that *they are not about the end of the world*. They are primarily concerned with events in the history of Israel and Judah, with warnings of disaster and promises of peace if the people repent. The third thing is that the prophetic call is to *renewed righteousness*; the message is primarily a moral one, not a set of precise oracular predictions about the future. The prophets of Judaism were proclaiming the moral demands of God, the judgment of God upon evil, and the promises of God, together with warnings about the price of disobedience as it is perceived in very specific historical situations.

Jesus stood firmly in this tradition. His message was urgent, for in historical terms the very existence of Israel and temple Judaism was at stake. His message was to Israel, but he apparently also saw the movement of the gospel message out beyond the boundaries of Israel to the nations.[13] Since his declared calling to was to "the lost sheep of the house of Israel," it seems likely that he would have been saddened at the thought that a Christian church might separate itself from the Jewish faith, and he would have been appalled at the thought that such a church might even become an enemy to Judaism.

THE TENANTS OF THE VINEYARD: The Jewish Heritage

> He began to tell the people this parable: "A man planted a vineyard, and leased it to tenants, and went to another country for a long time. When the season came, he sent a slave to the tenants in order that they might give him his share of the produce of the vineyard; but the tenants beat him and sent him away empty-handed. Next

11. Isa 58:6 and 7.
12. Amos 5:21–24.
13. E.g., Matt 8:11–12.

> he sent another slave; that one also they beat and insulted and sent away empty-handed. And he sent still a third; this one also they wounded and threw out. Then the owner of the vineyard said, 'What shall I do? I will send my beloved son; perhaps they will respect him.' But when the tenants saw him, they discussed it among themselves and said, 'This is the heir; let us kill him so that the inheritance may be ours.' So they threw him out of the vineyard and killed him. What then will the owner of the vineyard do to them? He will come and destroy those tenants and give the vineyard to others." When they heard this, they said, "Heaven forbid!" But he looked at them and said, "What then does this text mean:
>
> 'The stone that the builders rejected
> has become the cornerstone'?
>
> Everyone who falls on that stone will be broken to pieces; and it will crush anyone on whom it falls." When the scribes and chief priests realized that he had told this parable against them, they wanted to lay hands on him at that very hour, but they feared the people.
>
> —Luke 20:9–19

Jesus was very critical of the religious leaders of Israel. In the Parable of the Wicked Tenants (in all the Synoptics), the tenants of a vineyard beat and expel those sent to collect the rent. They even kill the son of the owner, so that they might claim the vineyard for themselves. Jesus asks what the owner would do about this, and gives (in Mark and Luke) or looks for (in Matthew) the answer that the owner will destroy the tenants and give the vineyard to others. The message seems to be that the religious leaders of Israel will be overthrown, and stewardship of the rule of God will be given to others, though it is not said who the others are. All the Synoptic Gospels add a quote from Psalm 118:22, to the effect that the stone the leaders reject will become the keystone of a new building. They interpret this to mean that Christ, the "rejected stone," will be the foundation of the new nation of the rule of God. In the hands of the Gospel editors, this parable seems to specifically speak of the church, a new community of the rule of God, founded on faith in Jesus.

This parable is, some commentators think uniquely among the parables, obviously an allegory. For that reason, Jülicher, who sharply distinguishes parables from allegories, thinks that it was invented by the church to show how the Christian church was the true heir of the kingdom. Dodd thinks it was original with Jesus, but, rather as in the Parable of the Sower, allegorical elements have been added by the church.[14] In its original form, he proposes that it was a challenge to his hearers to recognize the place of Jesus in Jewish tradition, and to face up to their responsibility to hear the message, and not "kill the son." Jeremias similarly sees the parable as defending Jesus' taking the gospel to the poor, as criticizing the religious leaders of Israel for failing to do so, and as warning that the poor would inherit the kingdom.[15] They both fail, however, to eliminate allegory even from their alleged original, since the parable does not make sense unless the vineyard tenants are seen as Pharisees, and the "others" are seen as the poor (or possibly the gentiles).

Crossan, as is his wont, proposes a very different interpretation, appealing to his reconstructed original version. He says that the vineyard owner is clearly foolish, as due to his thoughtlessness his son is killed, and the ownership of the vineyard is left in doubt. So in the original this was "a deliberately shocking story of a successful murder."[16] It had the function of shattering human wisdom and values, and forcing his hearers to consider what is right and just.

Scott goes back to a similar "original" version, stripped of allegedly later passages about the owner's repossession of the vineyard.[17] In that original, the parable has no closure or moral; the death of the son has no resurrection to give a happy ending. All the parable teaches is that God is willing to pay a price to achieve solidarity with ordinary humanity, but there are no supernatural miracles to be expected and no absolute moral certainties conveyed.

If you do not have an allergy to allegories, and if you think parables are polyvalent (can be properly interpreted in different situations to bring out different aspects of spiritual truth), it will be easier to accept church additions to an original parable, that help to interpret it afresh for their time. For instance, "killing the son," when spoken by Jesus, perhaps did not refer specifically to himself as Messiah, but emphasized the lengths to which wicked tenants would go to obtain the vineyard for themselves. Yet when Jesus was later recognized as "Son of God," who had actually been killed, it would be entirely natural to give a messianic interpretation to the parable.

14. Dodd, *Parables of the Kingdom*, 93–98.

15. Jeremias, *Rediscovering the Parables*, 57–65.

16. Crossan, *Power of Parable*, 96.

17. Scott, *Hear Then the Parable*, ch. 10.

The parable seems to be primarily a warning about the possibility that the kingdom would be taken from those who had killed the messengers of God (the messengers were surely the prophets), and given to others. It could well be a hidden proclamation (this would be the hidden mystery) of a new covenant community, indwelt and empowered by the Holy Spirit. Whether Jesus himself had said this specifically, or whether it was a later interpretation by members of the churches, it is in agreement with his teaching of the dawning of a new age of the rule of God.

For there was a new element in Jesus' teaching. He claimed that the time had come to fulfil the ancient prophecies. The rule of God had come near, and Israel, while it faced imminent destruction, was to be renewed in a new and unexpected way. The kingdom had already come in the person of Jesus. It was now to come, within the generation of those to whom he spoke, in a new more public form. It would not be a renewal of Israel as a political monarchy, but the birth of a community of a new covenant, a community of the Spirit.

One thing was perhaps unclear, but in view of what actually happened within Jesus' generation, it became apparent that this community would not be the full and final realization of the kingdom. The Crossan/Scott view, influenced by the work of the Jesus Seminar, significantly stresses this fact, that there was and will be no supernatural miraculous division of the pure from the impure at a specific point in human history. Yet they also seem to eliminate any positive element of moral teaching by Jesus, any possibility of positive divine action within history, and any hope for a fulfilment of a divine purpose of supreme value in some future state in which humans could share. However, I have tried to show that the parables speak of a consummation beyond history when all could share fully in the divine life, an ultimate realization of the kingdom, symbolized as a great feast with the patriarchs, prophets, and with the eternal Christ as King. As with the ancient prophets, the distinction between the coming of the new age of the Spirit and the ultimate consummation of history was blurred, and the two were run together in traditional symbolic imagery of renewal and fulfilment.

When the Synoptic Gospels were written, the ultimate consummation was still expected imminently by many. However, when pressed about when this would happen, the Gospels also record that Jesus always refused to answer, but instead spoke of the need for moral commitment and for that wider love of beauty and truth, for the appreciation of beauty and the understanding of nature, which is the heart of devotion to the Creator. He insisted that there would be judgment on what people had done in their lives, and a form of (corrective) punishment for evil, but the gospel, the good news, he brought was that there would always be hope for repentance and a joyful union with God. These things do not suggest an imminent "end of the world," but they do suggest the ending of the age of temple sacrifices and the beginning of a new age of life in the Spirit; they suggest a new view of human destiny as being that God wills all to share in the divine nature, which is unrestricted love; and they suggest an ultimate full realization of God's rule, however or whenever it would come about.

The destruction of the fig tree, the parable with which this section began, does refer to the destruction of Israel as a political entity and of the Jewish priesthood. But it should not be understood as the destruction of the divine covenant with the Jews, which will always remain in force.[18] It is the destruction of the temple in Jerusalem and its priesthood as social institutions. But the ancient covenant will never be rescinded, even though its outward forms may change. What Judaism preserves, and what it has given to the world, is awareness of the divine life within the heart, which was distinctive of the faith of Abraham, Isaac, and Jacob, but is also a light to the whole world. That promise must be spread throughout the whole world before the end of all things, and one vocation of the Christian churches is, not to oppose Judaism, or to undermine its distinctive way of life, but to expand the Jewish heritage to benefit the gentile world. The demand of unlimited love, the presence of that love within the heart, and the promise of sharing in divine love as the fulfilment of the world's life, that is the heart of the faith that Jesus, who was born and lived as a Jew, brought into the world.

THE GREAT FEAST: The Pharisees and the Jews; Some Unfortunate Negative Readings

> One of the dinner guests, on hearing this, said to him, "Blessed is anyone who will eat bread in the kingdom of God!" Then Jesus said to him, "Someone gave a great dinner and invited many. At the time for the dinner he sent his slave to say to those who had been invited, 'Come; for everything is ready now.' But they all alike began to make excuses. The first said to him, 'I have bought a piece of land, and I must go out and see it; please accept my regrets.' Another said, 'I have bought five yoke of oxen, and I am going to try

18. Rom 11:25–29.

them out; please accept my regrets.' Another said, 'I have just been married, and therefore I cannot come.' So the slave returned and reported this to his master. Then the owner of the house became angry and said to his slave, 'Go out at once into the streets and lanes of the town and bring in the poor, the crippled, the blind, and the lame.' And the slave said, 'Sir, what you ordered has been done, and there is still room.' Then the master said to the slave, 'Go out into the roads and lanes, and compel people to come in, so that my house may be filled. For I tell you, none of those who were invited will taste my dinner.'"

—Luke 14:15–24

The kingdom of heaven may be compared to a king who gave a wedding banquet for his son. He sent his slaves to call those who had been invited to the wedding banquet, but they would not come. Again he sent other slaves, saying, "Tell those who have been invited: Look, I have prepared my dinner, my oxen and my fat calves have been slaughtered, and everything is ready; come to the wedding banquet." But they made light of it and went away, one to his farm, another to his business, while the rest seized his slaves, mistreated them, and killed them. The king was enraged. He sent his troops, destroyed those murderers, and burned their city. Then he said to his slaves, "The wedding is ready, but those invited were not worthy. Go therefore into the main streets, and invite everyone you find to the wedding banquet." Those slaves went out into the streets and gathered all whom they found, both good and bad; so the wedding hall was filled with guests.

But when the king came in to see the guests, he noticed a man there who was not wearing a wedding robe, and he said to him, "Friend, how did you get in here without a wedding robe?" And he was speechless. Then the king said to the attendants, "Bind him hand and foot, and throw him into the outer darkness, where there will be weeping and gnashing of teeth." For many are called, but few are chosen."

—Matthew 22:1–14

The first stage of the kingdom is the new community of the Spirit on earth, the mediator of transcendence and liberation to a humanity estranged from God.

The second stage of the kingdom, where the patriarchs and the glorified Jesus himself live in the presence of God, is symbolized in terms of a great feast of joy and friendship. It is a present reality, though not in this spacetime, and it can be thought of as the highest level of the world to come, where beings are prepared for the third stage of the kingdom, the completion of the divine purpose for the cosmos, when all created things will be brought to share in the companionship of God.

Each stage of the kingdom is symbolized by a great feast, but there is something unexpected about the feast as it is represented in the first, earthly, stage. It is not to be identified in an unqualified way with any particular political or social or even ecclesiastical institution, and it consists of both good and bad, of beneficial and harmful, elements.

In the Parable of the Great Feast, according to Luke, a man prepared a great banquet and sent a servant to call those who had previously been invited to attend. But they made various excuses, saying they could not come. The host told his servant to bring into the banquet the poor, disabled, blind, and lame from the city streets. When there was still room available, he sent out his servant again to "compel" people to come in from the country roads and lanes. And he says, "None of those who were invited shall taste my dinner."[19]

Matthew puts it rather differently. It is a king who gave a marriage feast for his son.[20] The king sent many servants, but some of those who were invited beat and killed them. In response, the king destroyed those he had originally invited and burned their city to the ground. In Matthew's version, the host, being a king, more explicitly symbolizes God, and the servants seem to symbolise the prophets of Israel who were beaten or killed. Matthew explicitly says that those gathered from the city streets included both bad and good. And he adds, as if just to emphasize the point, that a guest who was not wearing a wedding-robe—presumably this is meant to convey that he was a bad one—was bound hand and foot and cast into outer darkness. At least he was not sent into the "fire" of Gehenna, where Matthew usually placed such people. In any case, for Matthew the moral is, "many are called but few are chosen."

The banquet is a frequent image for the kingdom of God. It is a time of fulfilment and happiness. But, explicitly in Matthew, Jesus speaks of the kingdom as it exists now on earth, for it contains both good and bad. Matthew sees the parable as referring specifically to Israel, to the way it had mistreated the prophets sent from God, and to the exile in Babylon. In Luke, Jesus' parable is related in reply to a man who remarked on the

19. Luke 14:24.

20. Matt 22:1–10.

blessedness of those who feast in the kingdom of God. In both cases, Jesus' issues a warning to those who are "heirs of the kingdom," the pious Jewish believers who assume they will be in the kingdom, to point out that the kingdom is already being given to others, for the pious have excluded themselves by their presumption and hypocrisy.

Scott sees the parable as a subversion of the honor system, and this is indeed a frequent theme of Jesus' teaching—those who rest on their privilege will be brought down, and those who make no such presumptions will be included in the kingdom.[21] The key question is, will this ever really happen? If not, the parable is fundamentally mistaken. If so, it is highly unlikely that it will ever happen in any actual human society on earth. Despite what Bernard Scott seems to imply, the parable thus essentially posits the kingdom as a future reality, but one in which the priorities and values of this world are reversed, and that must be a world radically different from this one.

Jesus teaches that those who presume they have God's favor because of their obedience to the letter of the Torah, may be excluding themselves from the kingdom. Because in the Gospels these hypocrites are frequently described as the "scribes and Pharisees," especially in Matthew, it is important to realize that being a scribe or a Pharisee is not in itself bad.

Dominic Crossan draws attention to the way in which the different Gospel writers deal with Jesus' criticisms of "the scribes and Pharisees." In Mark's Gospel, usually thought to be the first to be written, Jesus says "Beware of the scribes who like to walk around in long robes."[22] In English versions there is often a comma after scribes, which implies that we should beware of all scribes, and that all of them like to walk around in long robes. But that comma does not exist in the Greek text, so it is easier to see that Jesus is saying "Beware of those scribes who like to walk around . . . ." It is then not all scribes that Jesus is condemning, but only those scribes who are hypocritical. This becomes clearer in Matthew's version, when Jesus says, "I send you prophets and sages and scribes, some of whom you will kill and crucify."[23] Even Matthew sees that there are good scribes as well as bad, though his full account of this discourse of Jesus immediately blurs that distinction completely.

21. Scott, *Hear Then the Parable*, ch. 5.

22. Mark 12:38.

23. Matt 23:34.

In Mark, Jesus does tell his hearers to beware of those scribes and Pharisees who are arrogant and hypocritical, but all he says about them is that "they will receive the greater condemnation" (Mark 12:40). They will have to face the judgment of God. Luke's account is very similar; one of the things Jesus challenges is the use of religion to breed pride and extortion, and hypocrisy. When it comes to Matthew, however, Crossan points out that, according to Matthew, Jesus moves from making a challenge to hypocritical Pharisees to attacking the Pharisees as such.[24] And he does so in exactly the sort of language that Matthew's own "Sermon on the Mount" condemns.

So in Matthew's version Jesus says, "Woe to you, scribes and Pharisees, hypocrites."[25] He goes on to call them "blind guides," and ends by calling them "you snakes, you brood of vipers" and asks, "How can you escape being sentenced to Gehenna?" I think we have to see this account as an addition by Matthew himself, who repeatedly finds more angry and judgemental elements in Jesus' teaching. Like Crossan, I find it impossible to believe that if Jesus condemns those who call others "fools" or insults them,[26] he could himself have called the scribes and Pharisees snakes, vipers, and hypocrites. This is an example of Matthew's own judgemental attitudes. Unfortunately, it has led many Christians to be similarly angry at and judgemental of others. We need to go back to the Sermon on the Mount, and try to rid ourselves of all anger and prejudice in our dealings with others. If we do not, we will ourselves be exactly those sorts of "scribes and Pharisees"—that is, orthodox religious believers who totally break the second commandment to love our neighbors as ourselves—whom Jesus warns against.

A further argument against identifying the Pharisees with those forever excluded from the kingdom is that the Pharisees, or at least some of them, are, because of their pride and hypocrisy, among those who are lost to and alienated from God, even though they think themselves close to God. They are certainly lost sheep. We need to hold firmly in mind that Jesus' mission was to the lost sheep of Israel. It follows logically that his mission is to the Pharisees as well as to the tax collectors and sinners. Some Pharisees may be excluded from the kingdom, because of their pride and self-satisfaction. It needs to be said that some leading Christians will also be

24. Crossan, *The Power of Parable*, ch. 8.

25. Matt 23:13.

26. Matt 5:22.

excluded from the kingdom, and for similar reasons. They may, of course, be included in the earthly kingdom, which contains both bad and good. But they may, like the guest without a wedding-robe, be excluded from the kingdom in the world to come. Nevertheless, they will remain objects of God's unlimited love. We can only hope that they will, like the Prodigal Son, come to their senses, be welcomed back into the fold of the kingdom, and be the cause of rejoicing in heaven that those who were lost have been found.

An even worse example of Matthew's unfortunate legacy to Christian faith is that he, and he alone, has the crowd at Jesus' trial cry out, "His blood be on us and on our children."[27] This has led to the terrible belief that the Jews as such are responsible for the death of Jesus—a belief that almost certainly goes well beyond Matthew's intentions. That in turn has fed the vicious train of anti-Jewish propaganda that has disfigured the Christian church down the ages. It needs to be firmly kept in mind that the blood of Jesus does not call out for revenge. It is given for forgiveness. Unfortunately, the Gospel of John, which does not reproduce the speeches against the Pharisees in the Synoptic Gospels, but nevertheless records Jesus' very critical remarks about the scribes and Pharisees, speaks not only about the chief priests and the group of Jews who called for the death of Jesus, but writes that it was "the Jews" who called for his death. This is purely John's terminology, since Jesus would never have named his enemies "the Jews," if only because he was one.

Once again, the classification of a whole nation as enemies has had a terrible legacy in terms of encouraging anti-Jewish sentiments among Christians. This, despite the fact that Jesus and all his first disciples and followers were Jews, and most of them wished to remain so. And despite the fact that Jesus taught that his disciples should love their enemies.

What Jesus condemned was certainly not the Jews, and not those who killed him (since he asked for their forgiveness), and not the scribes and Pharisees as such. He condemned religious observance and belief as a cloak for self-righteous and judgmental attitudes, and for leading to hatred of infidels and heretics. In the Christian churches, the parallel would be people who proclaim their piety or their faith loudly while they support or incite hatred of gays and Muslims, for example. Such people may think they, and perhaps they alone, will inherit the kingdom, whereas in fact they have already excluded themselves from it. The key principle can be clearly stated:

27. Matt 27:25.

any group of religious people who think that they are morally or spiritually superior to others, and who espouse hatred, or even dislike, of "outsiders," are in fact unbelievers, infidels, in the deepest sense.

It is the outsiders who are brought into the banquet from the streets. The outsiders probably referred originally to socially undesirable Jews, whose presence would shock the self-righteously religious. When Luke's host sends out a second time, into the country, the "roads and lanes," this is usually taken to be a reference to gentiles, who, as would be clear by Luke's time, were flooding into the kingdom. This kingdom is not the final kingdom; there is judgment to come before that. Presence in it does not guarantee eternal life. Matthew's addition of the guest without a wedding robe makes that point with Matthew's typical brutality. We might well add that exclusion from the kingdom, the community of the Spirit, does not imply everlasting grief. The unnamed man in Luke's version of the parable—who petulantly vowed that no one he had originally invited would taste his banquet—is very unlike the God of Luke's Parable of the Prodigal Son, whose banquet would surely remain open to all who come to genuinely desire God's presence. For God's feast is incomplete until all who will are present. If any are excluded, it is because they do not really desire to be present.

Luke says that the servant should "compel" the country people (the gentiles) to come in, and this also has been a cause of some misunderstanding. Some have thought that it means compel *by force*, which would justify conversion to Christianity by threat or physical violence. This meaning is, however, not compatible with Jesus' teaching. He is very clear that we should always love our neighbor. Love entails respect for (not necessarily agreement with) the beliefs of others. Even if their beliefs differ importantly from yours, the whole idea of conversion by force is at odds with the command to love your enemies, do good, expecting nothing in return.[28] The thought that you might violently force others to believe what you believe is incompatible with such love.

It is a common but lamentable human practice to try to enforce uniformity of belief on a population. What that leads to is outward obedience to the social authority that does the enforcing, probably out of fear or timidity. Belief in God, however, is belief in something higher than any social authority, something that may be very critical of specific social authorities—like that of the Roman Empire or of its puppet ruler Herod, in Jesus' day. It is supremely ironic for a social or religious authority to try to impose

28. Luke 6:35.

a belief in God. A true belief in God is always liable to be critical of social authority, and a forced expression of belief is likely to breed resentment of the authority that imposes it, as well as skepticism about a belief that needs to be imposed by force.

Free personal assent is essential to religious faith. Compulsory belief is liable to be hypocritical belief, exactly the sort of belief that Jesus is objecting to. It is the heart that must be persuaded, and in the end it is only the Spirit of God that can move the heart, that can compel our assent, not by force but by love. We may rightly say that it is the vision of the overwhelming love of God that compels our assent to God's invitation. But we cannot physically or socially force that on anyone. The only compulsion that should be exercised by Jesus' disciples is the compulsion of a personal apprehension of truth and love. It is a Christian hope and prayer that in the end all will feel that compulsion, and will freely, and however late, share in the joy of God's banquet.

FOUR

The Moral Demand

THE RICH FOOL: The love of money

> Someone in the crowd said to him, "Teacher, tell my brother to divide the family inheritance with me." But he said to him, "Friend, who set me to be a judge or arbitrator over you?" And he said to them, "Take care! Be on your guard against all kinds of greed; for one's life does not consist in the abundance of possessions." Then he told them a parable: "The land of a rich man produced abundantly. And he thought to himself, 'What should I do, for I have no place to store my crops?' Then he said, 'I will do this: I will pull down my barns and build larger ones, and there I will store all my grain and my goods. And I will say to my soul, Soul, you have ample goods laid up for many years; relax, eat, drink, be merry.' But God said to him, 'You fool! This very night your life is being demanded of you. And the things you have prepared, whose will they be?' So it is with those who store up treasures for themselves but are not rich toward God."
>
> —Luke 12:13–21

THE RULE OF THE Spirit of God is like a joyful feast. But though joy is its predominant note, it also makes inescapable moral demands. It will be a community of perfected love. But love is hard to learn and to practice, especially for those who are estranged from God and trapped in pride, hatred, and greed. These entrapments are symbolized in the Gospels by the love of money. Those who love money love what they possess, and yet what they possess will pass away, and rarely brings what it may seem to promise.

Lovers of money tend to hate those who possess more than they have, and their greed is endless, for they always wish to possess more than they have.

The image of a "self-made man" is an image of a person who has accumulated many things, and whose self is constituted by those things. As those things pass away, so the self that sees itself as the owner of them also shrivels and dies. Jesus teaches that humans do not truly possess anything. All things are held in trust from God, and possessions and wealth are given so that we might use them wisely for the welfare of God's world. This is the moral demand that God places upon us, and there are few indeed who are able to respond adequately to it.

Jesus repeatedly teaches that one cannot serve riches and God.[1] He tells the story of a rich man who built bigger barns to store his increasing riches, and resolved to relax, to eat, drink, and be merry.[2] But that night he died, and he never enjoyed his riches. The moral is that it is better to be "rich towards God."

This is not a parable in the sense that it contains a deep mystery of faith. But it is mysterious, because it is extremely counter-intuitive, perplexing, and it leaves people with little idea of what they should actually do. Jesus said that it is harder for a rich person to get into heaven than it is for a camel to get through the eye of a needle.[3] But does that mean that it is bad to be rich or to aim at riches? And what does it mean to be rich towards God anyway?

The situation is much the same as that with the saying that one should not resist evil-doers.[4] A literal reading of this saying would leave us without armed forces or police. Thus, it seems to be hyperbole, an exaggerated saying that conveys a recommendation not to be vindictive, or not to use violence except as a last resort, and only when it can in the long run do more good than harm, and when it causes as little harm as possible. That is certainly how most Christians have interpreted it. It is still a saying with moral force, for it leads Christians always to avoid vengefulness and vindictiveness, even when evil-doers need to be resisted. But it is not to be taken literally.

A literal reading of the Parable of the Rich Fool might lead one to say that one should not be rich. But it is more likely to be condemning the

1. Luke 16:13.
2. Luke 12:13–21.
3. Matthew 19:24.
4. Matthew 5:39.

love of riches, or attachment to the luxuries that riches can bring. If wealth is lawfully gained, and if it is used for charitable purposes, there is nothing wrong with that—even the good Samaritan needed money to pay for the healing of the injured Jew. But then one is not pursuing wealth for its own sake, or for purely selfish purposes. Enormous good can be done with enormous wealth, and that is commendable.

What is to be avoided, then, is greed and undue attachment to wealth. But this saying too has teeth. How far can one live in luxury, drinking fine wines and eating exotic food, when so many people in the world are starving and homeless? If riches are justified only when used to promote good, how far can we use riches for our personal comfort, when there is so much good that calls out to be done?

We are to love our neighbor "as ourselves," which means that what we expect and do for ourselves we must be prepared to expect and do for others. As the Parable of the Good Samaritan tells us, our neighbors will include all other people, and maybe all sentient beings, and the planet itself, and especially all beings who are in need.

This is an extremely radical demand. It demands equal consideration for all, and it implies that we cannot keep for ourselves what could be used for others. There is clearly a problem, a problem about whether Christians should ever live more luxuriously than the poor of the earth, or if it is ever just to live comfortably while many others starve and die. The early Christians shared their goods in common. "No one claimed private ownership of any possessions, but everything they owned was held in common."[5] There were no people in need, for the disciples sold their lands and houses, and the apostles distributed the proceeds to anyone in need. It is said that dire consequences followed for two disciples, Ananias and Sapphira, when they held back just some of the proceeds of such a sale for their own use.

This passage should make any wealthy Christian of today pause. Throughout history, there have been relatively small Christian groups that have tried to live by sharing goods in common and doing without luxuries, from convents and monasteries to family communes. Even in such communities, however, there have often been arguments and divisions, and many of them have not survived for long. In the wider society, where not all are committed to Christian values, it is even less likely that such a way of life could be sustained without an iron social discipline, which would probably lead to repression and dictatorship. So it has become widely accepted that

5. Acts 4:32.

these communal ways of life are ideals for the few, not obligations for all. The problem of the right use of wealth remains, however, and it exerts an unremitting pressure on the consciences of Christian believers.

THE UNJUST STEWARD: God and Mammon

> Then Jesus said to the disciples, "There was a rich man who had a manager, and charges were brought to him that this man was squandering his property. So he summoned him and said to him, 'What is this that I hear about you? Give me an accounting of your management, because you cannot be my manager any longer.' Then the manager said to himself, 'What will I do, now that my master is taking the position away from me? I am not strong enough to dig, and I am ashamed to beg. I have decided what to do so that, when I am dismissed as manager, people may welcome me into their homes.' So, summoning his master's debtors one by one, he asked the first, 'How much do you owe my master?' He answered, 'A hundred jugs of olive oil.' He said to him, 'Take your bill, sit down quickly, and make it fifty.' Then he asked another, 'And how much do you owe?' He replied, 'A hundred containers of wheat.' He said to him, 'Take your bill and make it eighty.' And his master commended the dishonest manager because he had acted shrewdly; for the children of this age are more shrewd in dealing with their own generation than are the children of light. And I tell you, make friends for yourselves by means of dishonest wealth so that when it is gone, they may welcome you into the eternal homes.
>
> "Whoever is faithful in a very little is faithful also in much; and whoever is dishonest in a very little is dishonest also in much. If then you have not been faithful with the dishonest wealth, who will entrust to you the true riches? And if you have not been faithful with what belongs to another, who will give you what is your own? No slave can serve two masters; for a slave will either hate the one and love the other, or be devoted to the one and despise the other. You cannot serve God and wealth."
>
> —Luke 16:1–13

Other parables make similar points about the use of wealth. In one, a steward who was about to be dismissed for dishonesty, urgently (but dishonestly) reduces the debts his master is owed, so as to have friends when he loses his job. This passage in Luke is very obscurely written, perhaps because Luke has run together a number of apparently different sayings of Jesus in verses 9–13 (the second paragraph in the biblical text above), and appended them all to the parable as possible interpretations. It is a difficult parable, because the master (and therefore Jesus?) appears to commend the dishonest conduct of the steward. C. H. Dodd suggests that, just as the steward takes strenuous and decisive action to avoid the crisis of dismissal, so the disciples should act boldly in the crisis of the arrival of the kingdom and widespread opposition to it which will end in Jesus' death.[6] Jeremias suggests, similarly, that Luke has moved from Jesus' original "eschatological" emphasis (addressed to the crowd, urging them to act decisively in face of the coming crisis) to the "admonitory," especially in verses 9 to 13 (addressed to the churches, urging their members to act wisely in the use of money).[7]

Scott pays more attention to the problem created by the master praising an unjust person, and takes the parable to be a cryptic saying that challenges conventional ideas of the ultimate correlation of justice and power. The master, Scott suggests, may himself be morally corrupt and hard-hearted, and the steward's unjust actions are not punished. So there is a breakdown of the expectation that the just are rewarded and the unjust punished. The justice of the kingdom might not be a straightforward balance of action and reward, and God's justice might take more account of vulnerability, and the mixed nature of all human motives. The parable challenges any quasi-mathematical equation of goodness and reward, and might lead hearers to reflect on the ambiguity of all human actions, and the supra-moral nature of God's relationship to those actions. Even the unjust are accepted by God, and all divisions between the righteous and the unrighteous, or between the religious and the unreligious, are put in question.[8]

This interpretation requires disregarding the culminating sentence of the parable in Luke, "you cannot serve God and mammon," which does make a moral division between people, between those who love money and those who do not, and would thus undercut Scott's interpretation. But Scott takes verses 9 to 13 as additions made by Luke, not parts of the original parable. However, even if you take the original parable to end with the master's commendation of the unjust steward, the fact is that the steward is commended for his worldly wisdom, *not* for his dishonesty.

6. Dodd, *The Parables of the Kingdom*, 26.

7. Jeremias, *Rediscovering the Parables*, 34ff.

8. Scott, *Hear Then the Parable*, ch. 11.

It is one thing to say that God looks mercifully upon human actions, and quite another thing to suggest that God acts no differently towards those who defraud others than God acts towards those who are kind to others. Scott rightly defends God's mercy, but seems to overlook God's judgments, which are such a feature of many other parables (see, for example, the Parable of the Unmerciful Servant, considered in a later section, which declares, at least at first sight, that the unmerciful will be treated by God without mercy). It is right not to judge others harshly or to think that we ourselves are without fault, but in the parables generally there is a clear and decisive difference between just and unjust conduct.

I do not think the parable can be seen to be commending dishonest conduct. If, as Dodd and Jeremias hold, it warns people to act decisively and shrewdly in view of a coming crisis, it nevertheless cannot be recommending them to cheat and steal. A division remains between just and unjust, and no appeal to human solidarity can eliminate it. There is no reason why Jesus' call to act wisely should not extend to all disciples at all times, and as Jeremias admits, the change he supposes from "eschatological" to "admonitory," from action in face of a coming crisis in Israel to actions in the continuing life of the church, is more a change of emphasis than anything else. For the decisive action in face of the "crisis" of the coming of the kingdom does include being generous and charitable in the use of money. Above all, the steward's master commends him, not for dishonesty, but for "shrewdness" (*phronemos*—practical wisdom) and initiative.

The meaning seems to be that if the untrustworthy steward forgave debts, how much more would a loving God forgive the debts of his creatures. And how good it would be if the disciples were as shrewd as the steward, in their dealings with others. They could, for example, use what money (*mamona*, mammon) they have for just causes (helping the poor, for example). Then they might be welcomed in the world to come by those whom they have helped! (verse 9). Also, they should be faithful in small and worldly things (in the use of money) if they hope to be truly people of spiritual faith (verses 10–12). In fact, a good test of spiritual faith is found in one's use of worldly goods. It is no use praying often and being strictly religiously observant if one is not merciful and charitable in one's business and family life.

It does look as though Luke is running together a number of parables or sayings of Jesus, which are loosely connected by the idea of money and its use. That gives a confusing impression that makes this one of the most puzzling of parables. But I think it can be seen that Jesus is not praising shifty conduct, but wisdom, faithfulness, and charitableness in the use of money. There is little reason to doubt that the sayings, even if put together rather awkwardly by Luke, were original with Jesus. It does not seem that their meaning is limited to how the disciples should act in face of a coming crisis, as Dodd and Jeremias suggest. Whatever their original context, they are also universal teachings of wisdom for people in every time and place. They do not put all human moral intuitions in question, but recommend that Christian disciples should be as shrewd in their use of money as are dishonest and money-loving merchants.

As Jesus also said, a tree is to be judged by its fruits (Matthew 7:16). We cannot love God and love money. We should live in a trustworthy and benevolent way, especially in financial matters, regarding wealth as a gift of God to be used to promote general well-being, not as a possession to be used mainly for our own comfort.

THE RICH MAN AND LAZARUS: Dante's Gate

> There was a rich man who was dressed in purple and fine linen and who feasted sumptuously every day. And at his gate lay a poor man named Lazarus, covered with sores, who longed to satisfy his hunger with what fell from the rich man's table; even the dogs would come and lick his sores. The poor man died and was carried away by the angels to be with Abraham. The rich man also died and was buried. In Hades, where he was being tormented, he looked up and saw Abraham far away with Lazarus by his side. He called out, "Father Abraham, have mercy on me, and send Lazarus to dip the tip of his finger in water and cool my tongue; for I am in agony in these flames." But Abraham said, "Child, remember that during your lifetime you received your good things, and Lazarus in like manner evil things; but now he is comforted here, and you are in agony. Besides all this, between you and us a great chasm has been fixed, so that those who might want to pass from here to you cannot do so, and no one can cross from there to us." He said, "Then, father, I beg you to send him to my father's house—for I have five brothers—that he may warn them, so that they will not also come into this place of torment." Abraham replied, "They have Moses and the prophets; they should listen to them." He said, "No, father Abraham; but if someone goes to them from the dead, they will repent." He said to him, "If they do not listen to Moses

> and the prophets, neither will they be convinced even if someone rises from the dead."
>
> —Luke 16:19–31

In Luke's Gospel, the Parable of the Dishonest Manager is quickly followed by a much less puzzling story of an unnamed rich man and Lazarus, a poor man at his gate. The rich man is tormented in the flames of hades (the world of the dead), while Lazarus is taken to "Abraham's bosom," where there is apparently comfort and plenty of water.

To take this parable literally would be both nonsensical and morally opaque. Nonsensical, because Lazarus is presumably not literally lying on Abraham's chest. Morally opaque, because no reason is given for the difference in their treatments except that one was rich and the other poor, which does not seem of great moral relevance. Although Dominic Crossan thinks this is not primarily a moral tale,[9] but just a case of "role reversal," which makes hearers think hard about who they consider worthy of reward and punishment, I think it is reasonable to assume what the parable does not explicitly say, namely, that the rich man is guilty of ignoring the poor man at his gate, which is certainly morally relevant.

We have to read some other elements into the parable, drawing on a wider set of Gospel materials. Having done so, my interpretation is as follows: "Abraham's bosom" is a metaphor for an afterlife in the company of the patriarchs and prophets of ancient Israel—which is itself as metaphor for some form of communal existence after physical death in a spiritual realm. Lazarus must have been a man of great virtue, not just poor and possibly embittered and envious. We must assume that the rich man ignored the needs of the poor, which is why he is in torment. "The flames" represent the tortured mental agonies of a man who realizes that his whole life has been self-centred and loveless, so that he is no longer capable of love, and is cut off from the love of others and of God. The conversation between Abraham and the rich man is a literary device for making clear the existence of an impassable chasm between two different forms of afterlife, and the fact that these are consequences of the sort of life people had on earth.

An implication is that there is an afterlife in which individuals exist immediately after their physical deaths. They are not just waiting for a later resurrection and general judgment, as in Matthew 25, but are able to feel, think, and communicate. It is not anywhere in our spacetime. In the

9. Crossan, *The Power of Parable*, ch. 5.

world to come there are forms of punishment or reward for people's moral conduct on earth. Nothing is said, however, about how long the two states will remain separated by a great chasm, and the fact that the rich man is beginning to show some concern for his brothers may be a hint that the separation, and the punishment, will not last for ever.

Jeremias suggests that this should be called "the Parable of the Six Brothers,"[10] and that its main point is to warn luxurious livers of punishment to come. That seems unnecessarily whimsical. Yet it seems clear that Jesus teaches that there will be punishment for callousness and indifference, and that this is a serious matter. The moral demand of which this parable speaks is the demand not to ignore the poor who sit at the gate. This is not just because we will be punished after death if we do not. It is because everyone, however poor and wretched, is deserving of respect and care. Nevertheless, actions will have consequences, and if there is any cosmic justice, the way we have treated others will help to determine our own destiny.

The point mainly is that what one does in life will affect one's existence in a world to come, and that people will be judged according to their works.[11] It must be kept in mind, however, that Jesus teaches that callousness and indifference are vices. It is clear, then, that such qualities cannot apply to God. While God may punish (may place the dead in a position where they can begin to know and feel the harm they have done), God will always continue to wish for the ultimate good of every soul. The good news is that hope is not lost, even in the desolations of Hades. Dante's Gate, the one with "Abandon hope, all ye who enter here" written over it,[12] does not exist.

THE GOOD SAMARITAN: The extent of love

> Just then a lawyer stood up to test Jesus. "Teacher," he said, "what must I do to inherit eternal life?" He said to him, "What is written in the law? What do you read there?" He answered, "You shall love the Lord your God with all your heart, and with all your soul, and with all your strength, and with all your mind; and your neighbor as yourself." And he said to him, "You have given the right answer; do this, and you will live."

10. Jeremias, *Rediscovering the Parables*, 147.
11. Rom 2:6.
12. Dante, *Divine Comedy*, Canto 3 of "The Inferno" (trans. Henry Carey, 1814).

> But wanting to justify himself, he asked Jesus, "And who is my neighbor?" Jesus replied, "A man was going down from Jerusalem to Jericho, and fell into the hands of robbers, who stripped him, beat him, and went away, leaving him half dead. Now by chance a priest was going down that road; and when he saw him, he passed by on the other side. So likewise a Levite, when he came to the place and saw him, passed by on the other side. But a Samaritan while traveling came near him; and when he saw him, he was moved with pity. He went to him and bandaged his wounds, having poured oil and wine on them. Then he put him on his own animal, brought him to an inn, and took care of him. The next day he took out two denarii, gave them to the innkeeper, and said, 'Take care of him; and when I come back, I will repay you whatever more you spend.' Which of these three, do you think, was a neighbor to the man who fell into the hands of the robbers?" He said, "The one who showed him mercy." Jesus said to him, "Go and do likewise."
>
> —Luke 10:25–37

There are two parables that only occur in the Gospel of Luke, and they tell most vividly what love requires, and what the nature of God's love is. The first is the Parable of the Good Samaritan. The second is the Parable of the Prodigal Son, which I will consider later.

A lawyer, seeking to test Jesus, asks what he should do to inherit eternal life. Jesus asks him what is written in the Torah, and the lawyer gives two quotations from the Torah, "Love the LORD your God" (Deut 6:5) and "Love your neighbor as yourself" (Lev 19:18). Jesus replies that if one keeps these two commandments, one will live.

This entails that anyone who loves God and loves their neighbor will inherit eternal life, and is enough to refute the opinion that only those who overtly trust in Christ can do so. The test for gaining eternal life is simply love of God and of neighbor. Elsewhere in the New Testament, it is said that "everyone who loves is born of God" and that "if we love one another, God lives in us, and his love is perfected in us."[13] This needs a lot of unpacking, but it states that love of neighbor is enough to be born of God and to have God live in us, even if we say we do not believe in God. *Love is the ultimate criterion of true belief, and without it even belief that there is a God (and by implication belief in Christ) is not important.*

13. 1 John 4:7–12.

Love of our human neighbors is not, however, quite all that is required of us. Love of God is also required, a love with all your heart, soul, strength, and mind, that is, totally and with your whole being.[14] If you do not believe in God, it can seem hard to see how you can love God. Of course, you could not *explicitly* do so. But you can love *beauty*, in all its many forms; you can love *truth* and understanding of the complexity and intelligibility of the world; you can love our *world* and the living things that are in it; and you can love *justice* and *friendship*. Even though you might not believe in God, if God is the creator and giver of these good things, and if God is supremely beautiful, wise, loving, and just, then you may truly be said to love what God has in fact created, to love the works of God. It might also be said that, if you believed there was a God of supreme beauty, love, and wisdom, then you would naturally desire and love God. In a sense, this is a preparation for the love of God, and so it can be said that the love of beauty, truth, and goodness is what, even for atheists, can stand in for the love of God. It is a preparation for membership of the kingdom of God, and it is enough to make such membership possible if and when God is known as God truly is.

In the parable, the lawyer asks, "Who is my neighbor?" and Jesus tells a parable about a Samaritan—Samaritans were regarded as heretical aliens by Jews—who takes care of and pays for the recovery of an injured Jew, while a Jewish priest and a Levite have walked by on the other side. *He* is the neighbor, and he is an alien, even an enemy, not just someone of the same family, ethnic group, or faith. Dominic Crossan remarks that this is not an "example parable," which recommends being like a Samaritan, because Samaritans were traditionally disliked by Jews. It is rather, he says, a "challenge parable," which challenges traditional divisions of people into good and bad, and causes hearers to think again about their prejudices and discuss things further. For him, the final recommendation, "Go and do likewise" must be a Lukan addition to the original parable, which misses the purpose and intention of Jesus, which was to challenge the beliefs of his hearers.[15]

There is certainly a challenge in the parable; it challenges its hearers to regard traditional enemies as neighbors. But it also does so by giving a resounding answer to the question, "Who is my neighbor?" In the parable, it is someone usually regarded as an infidel or enemy. It is also someone whose actions provide an outstanding example of what is required of a good

14. Luke 10:27.

15. Crossan, *The Power of Parable*, ch. 3.

neighbor. The parable does not just say that people thought of as bad can be good. It says both "love your enemy" and "compassionate action towards even enemies (as in the Samaritan's care for a Jew) is what love requires." It also implies that infidels can be more loving, and so more acceptable to God, than the "orthodox." It is, in other words, both theological instruction (what God is like) and moral instruction (act like this).

Jesus does not directly answer the lawyer's question—he never answers trick questions that are meant to trip him up in some way. Instead, he tells a story about a traditionally hated class of person who goes to great lengths to help someone in need. This person cares for the well-being even of his traditional enemies. If he can do that, can I, who regard myself as good, do less? Jesus does not directly say who should be loved. Jesus' story implies that we should both help those in need and that we should learn to respect all humans, whatever their race or beliefs.

Is this to set us an example or is it to challenge our perceptions of who is good or bad? The genius of the story is that it is both. The lawyer is told to be like a Samaritan, a member of a hated community, which is undoubtedly a shock. He is also plainly told that this means doing good to enemies, and respecting those who have not previously been given moral consideration. The primary meaning of the parable is that we must extend the love we feel for our kin and community to include wider groups of people, whom we may not have previously considered or may even have demeaned. Crossan and Scott are right to say that the parable subverts conventional ideas of hierarchy and divisions between the orthodox and the infidel, or between one ethnic group and another. It is equally correct that this gives a moral teaching of a very definite and radical sort.

Further reflection on the parable, and on the Jewish tradition of loving one's neighbor, prompts even greater extensions of love. When God created the world, God saw that it was good. All animals are filled, as humans are, with "the breath of life."[16] Isaiah pictures the perfected life of the age to come as one in which "the wolf shall live with the lamb, . . . they will not hurt or destroy on all my holy mountain."[17] It is good that other animals than humans exist, and it is good that they should not be hurt or destroyed. Animals too should be loved and cared for, and because God has created them it is good that they exist and flourish, and that we should love them for what they are. We must care for everything that has the breath of life.

16. Gen 7:15.

17. Isa 11:6–69.

Humans are to have "dominion" over living things,[18] but it would be a terrible misunderstanding to think that such dominion means that we can do what we like with animals. Dominion is responsible care and protection, and it means fulfilling the divine will that all sentient beings, all beings capable of suffering and pleasure, should be the objects of human care and concern.

There is an even wider extension of love, for humans are also commanded to "till and keep" the Garden of Eden.[19] The garden is the earth, and it is to be cared for as we care for a beautiful garden. The love of the earth and of all that lives upon it is part of that greater love to which God calls us.

The Parable of the Good Samaritan calls us to extend love to the whole of creation, and tells us that such love is our greatest duty and responsibility. Faith in God is founded on the belief that there is a great moral purpose for creation. It is that all beings should find fulfilment and well-being, that the good potentialities of the world should be realized. God is the underlying Source of all things, who makes the realization of good possible, and who invites us to cooperate in bringing about that goal. God is the guarantor that there will be a final realization of goodness, in which God wills us to share.

These parables do not lay out a specific programme for how society in general should be organized. What they show is the personal moral orientation that should underlie all our decisions about social and political organization. They pose an alternative to any view that a person's moral beliefs are determined simply by their social or historical situation, and change wholly because of the changing of that situation. On the contrary, they state that individual hearts must first change, and that the principle of wisely ordered and universally extended love is absolute and unalterable. Difficult moral decisions in changing circumstances must still be made, and Jesus does not pretend to answer all our moral dilemmas in advance. Three principles, however, seem clear. First, the range of moral consideration must be worldwide, even though it seems right to pay primary attention to the needs of those closest to one, whether by chance or choice. Second, we must care for the needs of the poorest and least advantaged before we give preference to the rich and socially advantaged. Third, the love of wealth and luxury should not be adopted as a personal goal that is good in itself. At best wealth will be an instrumental good, and a means to

18. Gen 1:26.

19. Gen 2:15.

extending the common good for all people, so far as is possible. Jesus, it seems, always challenges the adequacy of our moral lives, but he does not resolve our moral problems for us. Above all, he leaves us in no doubt that we must do what God wants—which is the welfare of all sentient life—and not just what we want for our own well-being or the well-being of those with whom we are most closely associated.

FIVE

Judgement

THE FAITHFUL AND UNFAITHFUL SERVANTS: Judgement as Process

Who then is the faithful and wise slave, whom his master has put in charge of his household, to give the other slaves their allowance of food at the proper time? Blessed is that slave whom his master will find at work when he arrives. Truly I tell you, he will put that one in charge of all his possessions. But if that wicked slave says to himself, "My master is delayed," and he begins to beat his fellow slaves, and eats and drinks with drunkards, the master of that slave will come on a day when he does not expect him and at an hour that he does not know. He will cut him in pieces and put him with the hypocrites, where there will be weeping and gnashing of teeth.

—Matthew 23:45–51

"Be dressed for action and have your lamps lit; be like those who are waiting for their master to return from the wedding banquet, so that they may open the door for him as soon as he comes and knocks. Blessed are those slaves whom the master finds alert when he comes; truly I tell you, he will fasten his belt and have them sit down to eat, and he will come and serve them. If he comes during the middle of the night, or near dawn, and finds them so, blessed are those slaves. But know this: if the owner of the house had known at what hour the thief was coming, he would not have let his house be broken into. You also must be ready, for the Son of Man is coming at an unexpected hour."

Peter said, "Lord, are you telling this parable for us or for everyone?"

And the Lord said, "Who then is the faithful and prudent manager whom his master will put in charge of his slaves, to give them their allowance of food at the proper time? Blessed is that slave whom his master will find at work when he arrives. Truly I tell you, he will put that one in charge of all his possessions. But if that slave says to himself, 'My master is delayed in coming,' and if he begins to beat the other slaves, men and women, and to eat and drink and get drunk, the master of that slave will come on a day when he does not expect him and at an hour that he does not know, and will cut him in pieces, and put him with the unfaithful. That slave who knew what his master wanted, but did not prepare himself or do what was wanted, will receive a severe beating. But the one who did not know and did what deserved a beating will receive a light beating. From everyone to whom much has been given, much will be required; and from the one to whom much has been entrusted, even more will be demanded."

—Luke 12:35–48

Jesus teaches that God's love is unlimited, that God will never cease to care for those who seem lost to the presence and power of the divine. Jesus also teaches that God requires from us a passionate concern for the well-being of all. Failure to show such concern will inevitably result in judgement. Even though the judge will be the one who gave his life for those who have rejected God, there will still be judgement. In the Jewish and Christian traditions, the idea of judgement came to be symbolized by a decisive act of God in history, by which God eliminates evil and establishes *shalom*, the rule of justice and peace. In early Judaism, which had no very clear or universally accepted idea of life in the world to come, this was sometimes thought of as a future historical event, when the kingdom would be delivered to Israel, and all the nations would flock to the Jerusalem Temple to worship God.

Jesus did claim to fulfil the prophetic hope for the coming of one who would inaugurate this decisive event. But he also revised that hope radically, making it clear that his was not a political rule, and that it did not involve the destruction of Israel's enemies. To that end, he is reported as using the terms of Jewish apocalyptic thought—the symbolic imagery of a future decisive event in history—but giving them a different and more supra-historical reference. The parables to be considered next show this.

Jesus' parable of the faithful and unfaithful servants, as told in Luke and Matthew, provides an example. A faithful servant is described as one who rules the household in an efficient and caring way while the master is away. An unfaithful servant is one who beats the other servants and gets drunk. When the master returns, at an unexpected time, he will praise a faithful servant, but punish an unfaithful servant. Luke adds that the master will seat his servants at table and serve them—a wholly improbable occurrence, but within the magic world of the parable it makes the point that the master is Christ, the servant King, not an avenging warrior.

The parable is commonly taken to encourage the disciples to act responsibly while they wait for Jesus' unexpected return in judgement. Both Matthew and Luke insert the saying, "You also must be ready, for the Son of Man is coming at an unexpected time." This readily suggests the future historical interpretation of the parable. However, since it is a parable, a fictional story, the image of the absent and returning master may be seen as a device for warning that all human conduct in this life will be judged by God. Even if God seems absent, we should act as if "he might return at any time"—that is, as though God knows just what we are doing at every time, as in fact God does. It does not entail that Jesus or God will literally come to end history at any moment, as its context in the Gospels might seem to suggest. It fairly straightforwardly suggests that there will be judgement on how we act in life. The crucial point is that "you must be ready." It is an existential point, about how we should see each moment of our lives, not a prediction of some future event that is going to occur.

The mystery that is contained in this parable is that the symbol of an absent and returning master, which might seem to be saying something about a specific event in future history, is in fact about a continuing process in every present moment. Each moment is under divine assessment, and its consequences will be worked out beyond history, in a continuing process in the world to come.

Dodd and Jeremias both suggest that the parable originally made no reference to a delayed "second coming" of the Lord. The new age had begun with the life of Jesus, and faithfulness was needed because of the crisis that would be caused by Jesus' death and the growth of opposition to his disciples. They suggest that the unfaithful servant represents the religious authorities of Israel, who, if they do not look after those entrusted to their spiritual care, will be punished by being "put with the hypocrites" (Matthew) and "the unfaithful" (Luke). It was, they said, Luke and Matthew who re-interpreted this message so as to refer to a new future coming of the Son of Man, though Dodd adds that this re-interpretation is legitimate.[1]

However, since the parable is concerned with judgement, even if this judgement is seen as a continuing process, it is not one that is ever fully worked out within history. In this life, all the wicked do not get appropriately punished, and all the innocent are certainly not rewarded. If there is to be just judgement, it must be seen as taking place in some continuing process beyond this life. So even if Jesus did not literally refer to his return to earth in glory at some moment of historical time, it seems probable that he was referring to a post-historical process, one that culminates in encounter with Christ.

In Luke's telling of the parable, but not in Matthew's, Peter asks if this parable is "for us or for all." Does he mean to ask if this just concerns the disciples, or just the apostles, or the Jews as a nation, or even everyone on earth? Jesus' answer is very indirect. Just as Jesus answered the question, "Who is my neighbor?" by telling a story that implied that my neighbor may be someone I dislike (a Samaritan), so now Jesus answers the question, "Who will share in this new age?" by saying that "faithful stewards" are those who do not beat their servants, get drunk, and act unjustly. Those who act unjustly will be "cut in pieces"—lose their integrity, perhaps?—and will be put with the "unfaithful"—those who are untrustworthy and unloving. The severity of this metaphor is mitigated, in Luke's account, by the saying that those who know that what they are doing is "against their master's will"—i.e., is unjust—will receive a severe beating, while those who did not know that what they were doing was wrong will receive a light beating. It is hard to ignore the implication that there are different outcomes in the world to come, but that they will not endure for ever.

Jeremias thinks the parable applies especially to the apostles, who have special responsibility for the faithful.[2] By analogy with the Parable of the Good Samaritan, however, I rather think it implies that the new age of the kingdom is not just for the Jews (or even just for the Christians), but is intended for all who have the opportunity and responsibility to act justly. Thus, a question-mark is put against the view that in the coming of the kingdom Israel will triumph politically over all others. The parable also puts a question-mark for Christians over any claims that the Christian church will somehow be a politically powerful institution. The kingdom is

1. Dodd, *The Parables of the Kingdom*, 120.

2. Jeremias, *Rediscovering the Parables*, 44.

not literally an earthly monarchy, but it is a society of unrestricted neighbor love. Even when we take the parable to speak of a future fulfilment of the kingdom, Jesus never answers the question *when* this society will come—"It is not for you to know the times or periods that the Father has set."[3] Perhaps the reason is that in one sense it has already come in the person of Jesus; it is in process of coming, however fitfully and ambiguously, as the disciples learn to live in the power of the Spirit—"the kingdom of God is among [or 'within'] you";[4] and it will finally come only when the divine purpose for human history has been completed, when the universe has come to an end, an occurrence that is far beyond the comprehension of anyone at the time of Jesus, and even beyond anyone alive today.

THE TEN BRIDESMAIDS: Keep awake

> Then the kingdom of heaven will be like this. Ten bridesmaids took their lamps and went to meet the bridegroom. Five of them were foolish, and five were wise. When the foolish took their lamps, they took no oil with them; but the wise took flasks of oil with their lamps. As the bridegroom was delayed, all of them became drowsy and slept. But at midnight there was a shout, "Look! Here is the bridegroom! Come out to meet him." Then all those bridesmaids got up and trimmed their lamps. The foolish said to the wise, "Give us some of your oil, for our lamps are going out." But the wise replied, "No! there will not be enough for you and for us; you had better go to the dealers and buy some for yourselves." And while they went to buy it, the bridegroom came, and those who were ready went with him into the wedding banquet; and the door was shut. Later the other bridesmaids came also, saying, "Lord, lord, open to us." But he replied, "Truly I tell you, I do not know you." Keep awake therefore, for you know neither the day nor the hour.
>
> —Matthew 25:1–13

According to the Synoptic Gospels, Jesus believed that before the final realization of the kingdom there would be a time of judgement. This judgement would not, as many have thought, separate the faithful from the

3. Acts 1:7.
4. Luke 17:21.

unfaithful, but would apply even to those who regarded themselves as true believers. This is made clear in the Parable of the Bridesmaids.

This parable, found only in Matthew, tells of ten bridesmaids who went to meet a bridegroom. The bridegroom came at midnight, and it turned out that five of the women had forgotten to bring sufficient oil for their lamps. They went off to buy oil, but when they returned the groom and the other five had gone into the marriage feast. They were left outside, and the groom denied them entrance, saying, "I do not know you." Matthew concludes (even though all the bridesmaids had gone to sleep), "Keep awake, therefore, for you know neither the day nor the hour."

The novelist Philip Pullman has suggested that a better ending to this parable would have been for the bridesmaids with the oil to give some of it to the other five, so that they could all get into the feast. This is an appealing thought, though it misses the point that those who are not ready have excluded themselves from the feast, and they alone are responsible for being unready. No other human being can force you to be what you are not. The attitude of the groom may also seem uncharitable, but Jeremias suggests that the phrase, "I do not know you" referred to a Palestinian practice of excluding pupils from school for a week, not to a total and irrevocable ban.[5] Whether or not this is the case, the bridesmaids have certainly missed out on this feast, but we may think that they may have learned their lesson, and may be better prepared in future.

Both Dodd and Jeremias admit that the parable in the Gospels is used to refer to the coming of Christ in glory, but claim that in its original context the arrival of the bridegroom would rather have referred to a coming crisis for which Jesus' hearers should prepare themselves (perhaps the destruction of Israel, or the crucifixion of Jesus, or the persecution of early Christians, or even, more positively, the coming of the Spirit with power). The emphasis in Dodd and Jeremias is on being prepared for the coming of a great tribulation that will separate people into opposing camps. It has to be admitted that such a satanic and end-time tribulation did not occur, though the destruction of the temple and subsequently of Israel itself as a political entity may justly be seen as a catastrophe.

However, in any case, it seems that in the parable it is a wedding-feast that is being waited for, not an absolute disaster. The emphasis is on something good, though not all will be prepared for it. It might more justly be seen as the expectation of a new community of the Spirit. This was, as

5. Jeremias, *Rediscovering the Parables*, 138.

Jesus spoke, an imminent historical event, but the Gospel editors correctly thought that the Spirit continues to claim human lives throughout history, so that the command to "be prepared" applies to the new Christian community too. I think Dodd and Jeremias were right in not tying the parable to some specific future ending of history, but there seems little reason for tying it too tightly to particular events in the history of Israel.

Throughout human history, those whose hearts are prepared will enter into the heavenly feast in the world to come, while many whose hearts are not prepared will exclude themselves from that community. Since all ten women were bridesmaids, they were people who intended and expected to go to the feast, but turned out not to be genuinely prepared. They thought they were in the kingdom, but actually they were not all ready. The reference could originally have applied to the Pharisees, Jeremias suggests, though by extension it would apply to religious people of all sorts at many times, especially Christians who presume that they are "saved" or are safely in God's kingdom.

The parable does not entail that such people are altogether and forever excluded from the presence and love of God. Nor is it a prediction that some people will definitely be excluded from the kingdom. It is rather a warning of a possibility that can and should be avoided if appropriate action is taken. The trap some Christians fall into is that of thinking that there is one and only one invitation to the eternal feast, that some people will definitely be excluded, and that the consequences of being included or excluded are absolute and irreversible. Such a view neglects entirely any belief in the enduring and patient love of God, and it overlooks Jesus' radical revision of the idea of the Messiah and of the kingdom. If it is thought that the Messiah will not come to establish the state of Israel as the kingdom, but to establish the rule of the Spirit in human hearts, then the idea that there is just one catastrophic event that will be decisive for the whole of history loses its appeal. There is good reason to think that the kingdom of the Spirit will always remain open to those who will prepare themselves for it, and there is little reason to think that people will only get one chance to enter the kingdom.

It is true that, in the symbolism of the parable, there is only one feast and one bridegroom. But this parable only focusses on one aspect of the spiritual life, the need for preparation. It needs to be complemented by parables of repentance, like the Prodigal Son or the Lost Sheep, which show that even the lost and excluded will find a joyful welcome when they come to their senses. Exclusion is real; but if God is indeed a God of love no exclusion is permanent and irrevocable.

MONEY LEFT IN TRUST: use your gifts

As they were listening to this, he went on to tell a parable, because he was near Jerusalem, and because they supposed that the kingdom of God was to appear immediately. So he said, "A nobleman went to a distant country to get royal power for himself and then return. He summoned ten of his slaves, and gave them ten minas, and said to them, 'Do business with these until I come back.' But the citizens of his country hated him and sent a delegation after him, saying, 'We do not want this man to rule over us.' When he returned, having received royal power, he ordered these slaves, to whom he had given the money, to be summoned so that he might find out what they had gained by trading. The first came forward and said, 'Lord, your mina has made ten more minas.' He said to him, 'Well done, good slave! Because you have been trustworthy in a very small thing, take charge of ten cities.' Then the second came, saying, 'Lord, your mina has made five minas.' He said to him, 'And you, rule over five cities.' Then the other came, saying, 'Lord, here is your mina. I wrapped it up in a piece of cloth, for I was afraid of you, because you are a harsh man; you take what you did not deposit, and reap what you did not sow.' He said to him, 'I will judge you by your own words, you wicked slave! You knew, did you, that I was a harsh man, taking what I did not deposit and reaping what I did not sow? Why then did you not put my money into the bank? Then when I returned, I could have collected it with interest.' He said to the bystanders, 'Take the mina from him and give it to the one who has ten minas.' (And they said to him, 'Lord, he has ten minas!') 'I tell you, to all those who have, more will be given; but from those who have nothing, even what they have will be taken away. But as for these enemies of mine who did not want me to be king over them—bring them here and slaughter them in my presence.'"

—Luke 19:11–27

For it is as if a man, going on a journey, summoned his slaves and entrusted his property to them; to one he gave five talents, to another two, to another one, to each according to his ability. Then he went away. The one who had received the five talents went

> off at once and traded with them, and made five more talents. In the same way, the one who had the two talents made two more talents. But the one who had received the one talent went off and dug a hole in the ground and hid his master's money. After a long time the master of those slaves came and settled accounts with them. Then the one who had received the five talents came forward, bringing five more talents, saying, "Master, you handed over to me five talents; see, I have made five more talents." His master said to him, "Well done, good and trustworthy slave; you have been trustworthy in a few things, I will put you in charge of many things; enter into the joy of your master." And the one with the two talents also came forward, saying, "Master, you handed over to me two talents; see, I have made two more talents." His master said to him, "Well done, good and trustworthy slave; you have been trustworthy in a few things, I will put you in charge of many things; enter into the joy of your master." Then the one who had received the one talent also came forward, saying, "Master, I knew that you were a harsh man, reaping where you did not sow, and gathering where you did not scatter seed; so I was afraid, and I went and hid your talent in the ground. Here you have what is yours." But his master replied, "You wicked and lazy slave! You knew, did you, that I reap where I did not sow, and gather where I did not scatter? Then you ought to have invested my money with the bankers, and on my return I would have received what was my own with interest. So take the talent from him, and give it to the one with the ten talents. For to all those who have, more will be given, and they will have an abundance; but from those who have nothing, even what they have will be taken away. As for this worthless slave, throw him into the outer darkness, where there will be weeping and gnashing of teeth."
>
> —Matthew 25:14–30

If the possibility of exclusion from the kingdom of the world to come is real, the parable of the *talents* provides one reason for such exclusion. This parable is more accurately a parable of money left in trust for trading. It is given, in slightly different versions, in both Matthew and Luke. It is introduced in Luke as a response to the disciples' belief that the kingdom was about to come immediately. In Luke's version, a nobleman going to be crowned as king leaves ten *mina* (about three month's wages for a labourer) with his servants, to be invested by them in trade. When he returns as king he calls them to account. He rewards those who have increased their capital, but condemns one who had not put his money to work, but just wrapped it in a cloth. The culprit is deprived of his money, and it is given to the one who had traded most profitably. Then the King slaughters those who had meanwhile hated him and tried to reject his kingship. The reference to a king makes this an explicitly messianic parable. The slaughter of the king's enemies may refer to the imminent destruction of Jerusalem. The main point of Luke's narrative is that the king is absent (the kingdom will not come immediately, since the nobleman has gone to "a far country"), but will return to call his servants to account.

Matthew gives a rather different account, though it is also embedded in a messianic passage about the "coming of the Son of Man." The man who goes on a journey is not a king. He gives different amounts of money to each servant, but each man gets a huge amount (even one *talent* is worth more than fifteen years wages for a labourer, and he gives out between one and five *talents* each). The servant who did not use his money for trade, but hid it in the ground, was told that he should have invested it in a bank, and is then "cast into outer darkness."

The differences between the accounts in Matthew and Luke show that these are not exact translations of Jesus' Aramaic words, but they add some interpretations characteristic of the Gospel editors themselves. It also seems clear that the editors have chosen to put together various remembered sayings of Jesus to make a connected narrative, and that the connections are sometimes very strained. Nevertheless, the collected parables have a consistent set of teachings, and a unique and vivid style, which makes it highly probable that they did originate, in some form, with Jesus.

Crossan points out that it is virtually impossible to capture exactly what Jesus originally said, and he may anyway have used the parable in various forms on various occasions. The basic structure is that of an absent and returning master, who will assess people on the use they have made of what he gave them in trust.

It seems that Jesus' concept of messiahship was not that of a sudden and violent overthrow of the enemies of Israel, even though the writer of the second letter to the Thessalonians still toys with such a notion.[6] That leads one to ask whether the thought of a sudden return, ending the normal run of human history, is to be taken literally. We cannot answer that question definitively. But the fact that Jesus speaks in parables (poetic images in narratives that are fictions with a spiritual meaning) implies that

6. 2 Thess 1:7 and 8.

if their meaning is spiritual, it may not primarily refer to specific historical events at all.

Historical events may be symbols for spiritual processes. There was no nobleman who went away for "a long time."[7] There were no servants who traded with the money he had left them. The master did not return as a king who slaughtered his enemies. It is left to the hearers to decide what the spiritual meaning of this story is, and we might do well to remember Jülicher's warning against excessive allegorization. Not every element of the story will map onto some spiritual fact. The general structure of the parable—a structure of absence, return, and reward or retribution—is what is most important. The idea of absence emphasizes our responsibility for our actions—not a specific event of departure, but a continuing sequence of actions. The idea of return emphasizes our accountability—not an event when a specific judgment is made, but a continuing placing of our actions in the light of eternal values. The idea of reward or retribution suggests not a specific penalty for a specific crime, but a future spiritual process in which the consequences of our actions and attitudes are worked out.

Partly because the word *talent,* which is a large sum of money, in English refers to a skill or ability, this parable has been widely taken to commend using one's gifts as fully as possible. The person who is punished is someone who does not use his gifts. Dominic Crossan holds that this is an "incorrect" interpretation.[8] He points out that the vineyard owner is described as hard and severe—hardly a symbol for God. And one servant was punished for not lending money at interest, though taking interest is prohibited by Jewish law—so he ought to have been commended. Therefore, the parable is not commending either the owner or the rewarded servants, but is a challenge to its hearers to think about their attitudes to greed and social justice. Is it right for masters to be hard and severe? Is it right to lend money at interest? The aim, Crossan thinks, is to subvert our accepted values and make us think again about them, and come to our own decision. Maybe we should think that normal standards of reward and punishment are perverse, and do not reflect the values of the kingdom. Parables like this aim, Crossan says, to shatter the complacency of one's world, and introduce us to a new "world" where we can be encouraged to act boldly and in freedom.

7. Matt 25:19.

8. Crossan, *The Power of Parable*, ch. 5.

The difficulty with that interpretation is that it seems to imply that there are no eternal values rooted in the being of God that are binding on us whatever we think. It is good to be critical and reflective, but there are some positive values that we ought to accept and act on. Also, I would think that the "world" to which the parables introduce us is not just a new way of seeing things in this world, but an existing spiritual reality in which we can grow and learn, already in this life and importantly after physical death.

In my judgement, the remarks about the severity of the master and the possibility of lending at interest are secondary features of the parable that have no spiritual significance. What is significant is the point about making money by trading, something that the fearful servant failed to do. The central feature of the parable is about employing money to do useful work. Money is a natural symbol for the gifts God has given, and what is condemned is keeping those gifts to oneself and not putting them to use at all. Money can therefore represent abilities that one has (it is not just that the word "talent" in English means ability!), so the parable is, as Matthew and Luke assume, about using one's abilities for good (being fruitful) or just letting them lie fallow. It suggests that there really will be a future, though I would think not in the history of this world, when the master, the giver of gifts, is seen to be present, and when the just consequences of our acts in this world are worked out. What matters in the present is that disciples of Jesus must be active in goodness, especially towards the poor, the starving, the sick, and the imprisoned. Merely to proclaim one's faith and obedience to religious rules is worse than useless.

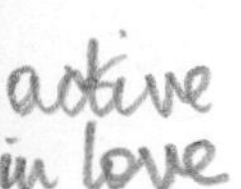

THE UNJUST JUDGE: the coming of the Son of Man

Then Jesus told them a parable about their need to pray always and not to lose heart. He said, "In a certain city there was a judge who neither feared God nor had respect for people. In that city there was a widow who kept coming to him and saying, 'Grant me justice against my opponent.' For a while he refused; but later he said to himself, 'Though I have no fear of God and no respect for anyone, yet because this widow keeps bothering me, I will grant her justice, so that she may not wear me out by continually coming.'" And the Lord said, "Listen to what the unjust judge says. And will not God grant justice to his chosen ones who cry to him day and night? Will he delay long in helping them? I tell you, he

> will quickly grant justice to them. And yet, when the Son of Man comes, will he find faith on earth?"
>
> —Luke 18:1–8

Judgement and the vindication of the just will come, but human history will continue in its ambiguous juxtaposition of moral heroism and depravity. In view of this, Jesus told the disciples a parable "about their need to pray always and not to lose heart." He tells of a judge who listens to a widow's requests for justice and vindication (perhaps for the remission of an alleged debt) just because she is so boringly repetitive and insistent. If even an unjust judge does this, he says, how much more will God hear the prayers of those who cry for justice and vindication. God will do so "quickly."[9] That is, God will respond at once. There will be a vindication of those who cry for justice.

There is a distinct oddity about this parable. Not only is the judge in the parable lazy and indifferent to others, the widow is tiresome and selfish, since she asks only for justice for herself, not for others. Obviously, Jesus is not commending such attitudes. He says, if even such a lazy judge will respond to calls for a declaration of innocence in the face of accusations from an enemy, or for a remission of a debt, God will surely vindicate or justify—in Gospel terms, make righteous or treat as righteous—those who pray for vindication, and God will do so "quickly," that is, immediately or without delay.

When it comes to the widow, it should be said that the prayers of believers should not only be for a rather self-centred declaration of innocence for them in the face of vilifications by their critics. They should be prayers for true justice for all in the face of persistent injustice in the world. Jesus' assurance is that justice will be done, even though that may not be obvious within the course of history. God's actions will need to leave the moral freedom of humans intact, and so they will not be as obvious and dramatic as some might hope. Yet God will act, often in unexpected or in hidden ways, to influence events, both to inspire actions for the sake of goodness and also so that evil will not overwhelm the good. And God will ensure that in the end justice will be done

From its context in this Gospel, we can see that Luke probably thought there would be a specific day of decisive judgement that would come very soon. But that would be a reversion to the political view that Jesus had in

9. Luke 18:8

general renounced, as well as being in tension with other parts of Luke's Gospel, which stress the present reality of the kingdom. The parable itself does not entail a quasi-political view of the triumph of Israel over her enemies. It is more concerned with the fact that God will vindicate, will make righteous, and that prayers to God will never be in vain. Vindication could have been seen by Jesus' hearers in the descent of the Spirit upon the disciples at Pentecost, which was for them in the near future, and which brought both justification in the sight of God and freedom from the domination of sin. For us, the gift of the Spirit is also something that may come upon us swiftly, and it brings justification and forgiveness from God. Disciples ought never to lose heart or lose sight of this fact.

Luke appends to the parable the saying, "When the Son of Man comes, will he find faith on earth?"[10] In its main Old Testament occurrence, the expression "one like a son of man" is used in the book of Daniel as a symbol not primarily of an individual, but of a group or community, "the holy ones of the most High,"[11] who would usher in the rule of justice and mercy, which will supplant the rule of four beasts from the sea, sometimes taken to symbolise the militaristic empires of Babylon, Media, Persia, and Greece. Just as the beasts are symbols of nations, so the "one like a son of man" is a symbol of a community. It is the symbol of the new community of the Spirit, in which humans will live in universal peace and friendship with God and with one another. As has been noted, this community is already established in "heaven," in the feast of the King with Abraham and the prophets. On earth it exists, but only in a fitful and ambiguous way, in the hearts of men and women.

Jesus could have referred to himself as "Son of Man" (the Gospels say he did), meaning that he would inaugurate this new community of peace and righteousness, destined to supplant the militaristic power of the Roman Empire. This would be a new age, ending the age of temple sacrifices, and also ending the existence of Israel as a political entity, and later of Rome, as worldly powers. Jesus' mission was to turn Jews to the true and inward worship of God instead of relying on external conformity to the divine Law, and to enter into the new age of the kingdom of God.

On this interpretation, the coming of the Son of Man is the coming of the rule of those who are sanctified by God, and that rule is not a political rule that dominates others, but the rule of love, an inward reality in the

10. Luke 18:8.

11. Dan 7:13–14 and 7:18.

heart and an attempt, always ambiguous and imperfect, to create a society in which the master-slave relationships of the social order of Jesus' day are overturned. This will be a new age and a new social order, and the disciples are to prepare themselves for it.

Yet that new age is probably never to be fully realized within human history. It can only be completed in the world to come, and it will only become universally apparent in the final restoration of all creation. In one sense, the Son of Man has *already* come in the glory of the Father, in the sense that Jesus, by his resurrection and ascension, has been glorified and transfigured in God's presence. In another sense, the Son of Man will finally come in glory and be seen and acknowledged by all in the days of the new creation of heaven and earth, the end and goal of all things. In a third sense, in this world, talk of the coming of the Son of Man is a symbol for the immanent presence of the glorified Christ in the community of the Spirit.

Early Christians like the editor of Luke's Gospel tended to see the coming of the Son of Man as a historical event, probably in the near future. But they also knew that there was a Christian calling to proclaim the love of God in Jesus to the gentiles, that the kingdom was destined to grow throughout the whole world, and that the kingdom as it was being experienced by the disciples of Jesus was far from being a perfect society. In view of these things, the thought that Jesus would literally return to earth in glory very soon began to seem increasingly unrealistic. It became more obvious that to speak of "the coming of the Son of Man" is to speak of the events of this world as seen in the light of the demand and promise of the ultimate goal of humanity, embodied in the present reality of the glorified Christ. The present reality of Christ is also the lure of the future goal of humanity, and ultimately of all creation. It comes as an invitation to the realization of future goodness, which calls for a response of trust and commitment.

When it is asked whether the coming Son of Man would find faith on earth, this is not about a future historical event in which Jesus finds out what is happening on earth. It is about the existential state of humanity, in face of the pressing moral demands of the kingdom. In a world dominated by hatred, greed, and ignorance, there is a desperate need for a power of goodness that will save our world from chaos and destruction. There remains a possibility that even the disciples of Christ might desert and deny him (as Peter did after the crucifixion). The disciples are challenged to remain true to their experience of the love of God in Christ, even in times of persecution and hardship.

Seen thus, the parable calls for persistent prayer for spiritual, not political, justification. It is not implying that God will vindicate Israel as a political state against her enemies. Jesus is declaring that God will justify his disciples—will treat them as righteous, and ultimately make them righteous—though their conduct and their consciences, as well as their enemies, may accuse them. We need to be persistent in prayer, even in time of difficulty and discouragement, for God to enable us to share in the Spirit of Christ, to have our sins forgiven, and to grow into his image. This is a parable of life in the Spirit, not a parable of political revolution.

PARABLES OF JUDGEMENT: Be prepared

Commentators like C. H. Dodd hold that parables of judgement, as spoken by Jesus, would not have originally referred to a final return of Christ in glory at all.[12] They are later attempts, after Jesus' death and resurrection, to account for why the kingdom had not yet come in its fullness, and to adjust the remembered parables to make them refer to an expected yet delayed return. Dodd argued that Jesus would have had no such belief, but was speaking of the crisis caused by his teaching, especially his criticisms of the religious authorities of his day. He was warning his disciples to "be prepared," and to pray without losing heart, because his teaching would cause a division in Israel, which would separate those who accepted his teaching and those who did not. The disciples would have to be prepared for such a crisis.

Though it is true that this teaching of an "unexpected return" is not the major element in the parables, it is hard to think that it would not have been present in the teaching of Jesus at all. After all, Professor Dodd accepts that Jesus could have spoken of the future, and could have foreseen a terrible judgment upon Israel.[13] He could well have foreseen his probable death at the hands of his enemies, and this would have caused a crisis for the disciples. As Dodd accepts, it is also likely that he could have looked for some form of vindication by God, and this vindication, manifested in the resurrection and the Pentecostal experience of the Spirit, Dodd thinks, would itself be the "coming of the Son of Man" to which the parables originally referred.

12. Dodd, *The Parables of the Kingdom*, ch. 7.

13. Dodd, *The Parables of the Kingdom*, 45ff.

Nevertheless, if this is, as Dodd seemed to think, all that talk of the "return" of Christ has to say, it seems to deprive the disciples of any real future hope. If the kingdom had arrived, and if that is all it was, and if one result of it was that Jesus would die and the disciples would be persecuted, that is not very hopeful. If human destiny is to live with God for ever, that is a real hope, but it must be in some real sense *future*. It may indeed be in a world to come—an idea that was by Jesus' time a fairly widespread, though not universal, belief in Judaism, apparently shared by Jesus—but it is still a future form of human existence.

Since Jesus was seen alive after his physical death, there obviously was a world to come in which Jesus continued to exist in a transfigured form. The disciples' hope would be to share in this life. In other words, the hope was that in their post-death existence Jesus would appear to them in glory.

Furthermore, their hope was not just that they themselves would encounter Jesus after their deaths, but that every personal creature might be part of that heavenly kingdom. There would be a sharing of all created things in the divine life. Though they could have had no idea of the vastness of God's creation, they did believe that there were many spiritual entities of different sorts (angels, for instance) in existence. Similarly, they had no idea what a resurrected body would be like, but they believed that somehow there would be a shared communal existence of all created things in God. Such things could not be literally described—"what no eye has seen, nor ear heard, nor the human heart conceived . . . God has prepared for those who love him."[14]

Thus, there was a hope for something beyond Jesus' resurrection and their present form of life. It would be strange if this had not been part of Jesus' teaching. And such things were spoken of in the traditional symbols of prophecy—a great throne of judgment, a return on the clouds, a new heaven and earth, an elimination of satanic evil. The symbols are not to be taken literally, for nothing literal would be adequate to describe what no heart could conceive, but they do symbolize something future and something real. The appropriate action in view of such a hope is to be prepared and to be active in doing good.

Professor Dodd does speak of a trans-historical existence,[15] and he does stress that the kingdom has come near in Jesus and the community of the Spirit of Christ. This is helpful, but there is no need for him to deny that

14. 1 Cor 2:9.

15. Dodd, *The Parables of the Kingdom*, 79 ff.

Jesus could also have spoken both of his continuing presence in that new community and of his eternal existence in the presence of God. John's Gospel explicitly asserts these things; they are things a person who experienced a strong sense of union with God and a calling to found an expansion of Judaism, a community of the Spirit, would almost certainly have believed; and they are things that the parables can be seen to express in seemingly simple stories that contain mysteries that need to be decoded.

If I am right, many Christians are mistaken in thinking that there is an everlasting hell from which there is no redemption, in thinking that Christ might literally return to this earth in glory at any moment, and in thinking that only those who during their lifetimes explicitly believe in Christ will enter into eternal life. These mistakes are derived from the fact that Jesus did proclaim judgment on evil, that he did see one temporal image of such judgment expressed in the imminent historical events of the destruction of Jerusalem and the temple, that he believed that he would be seen by his disciples in the glory of the Father, and (if we add John's Gospel to the accounts) that he taught that the way to eternal life for humans was by belief in the Son of Man as the human incarnation of God.

Early Christians accepted that these things were true, but I think that many early disciples failed to see the most fundamental radical teaching of Jesus, namely that God was a God of unlimited mercy and love. When Matthew writes, 'Be perfect . . . as your heavenly father is perfect,"[16] he has outlined what that perfection is in the collection of sayings that forms the "Sermon on the Mount." It includes loving your enemies,[17] not resisting evildoers,[18] and renouncing anger.[19] If these are moral ideals for humans, and if humans are to be like God, then God must care for enemies, never wholly reject evildoers, and always be prepared to overcome anger with love. And that is precisely what Jesus' sermon claims. Consequently, judgment could not be the last word in God's relations with sinful humanity, and there would have to be a time, not measurable in human terms, in which God could bring alienated humanity into true and loving union with the divine. Only then could the process of salvation, of sharing in the divine nature, be complete, so that Christ could appear in glory and be acknowledged by all.

16. Matt 5:48.

17. Matt 5:44.

18. Matt 5:39.

19. Matt 5:22.

The idea of an imminent return of Christ to this earth that would put an end to all human development almost inevitably led to the idea that millions would be condemned to exclusion from eternal life with God. If this is found to be unacceptable, then the idea of a "second coming" in the near future on this planet must be abandoned.

However, it remains true that we, even now, have no idea of when life on this planet will end. We know it will end sometime, and most of us hope that it will not be very soon. But it could indeed be tomorrow. If that happens, there will still be life in the world to come. It will not cut off all hope of development, repentance, and spiritual growth for those who have entered into the world to come. But it will cut off human possibilities for moral and spiritual decision-making in this world, decision-making that determines the form of afterlife into which humans will enter. For that reason, disciples should "stay alert," living as if Christ may return at any moment. Though Christ's return in glory will in fact be beyond this world's time altogether, yet it will happen.

Since our actions now will determine our other-world destiny for incalculable ages, it is a good spiritual practice to constantly think of Christ's return as if it could happen at any time. This is an imaginative device for cultivating spiritual and moral endeavor. It is rather like saying, "Live every day as if you are about to meet the person you most respect in the world." That would keep us bright and on our toes. And that is the way we should live. Since Jesus is in fact in paradise now, and his Spirit is in our hearts, and since the eternal Word exists at every time, this will not be just an illusion. It is a way of making that presence psychologically real to us, and thinking of the promise of its full realization as the ultimate goal of our created lives.

There are three main things to learn from the group of parables of judgement and the coming of the kingdom. First, that even among the closest disciples, there were misunderstandings of Jesus' teaching and of his place in the purpose of God. The revelation of truth in Jesus did not come as a final, completed, inerrant, and consistent totality. What the Gospels reveal is what was remembered of the life and teachings of Jesus, the impact of his person on the disciples, and a witness to his resurrection. The Gospels clearly show that Jesus was often misunderstood. Jesus himself was remembered as strongly believing in an imminent judgment on Israel, in the need for repentance and trust in God, and in the ultimate triumph of goodness. But he consistently avoided questions about when and exactly how this would be, and instead stressed the importance of a just and compassionate life. Christian faith is not the possession of infallible information about exactly what would happen next in history, but a present commitment to goodness and trust in its ultimate realization.

Second, many parables are very difficult to understand, and need to be interpreted in the light of the whole story of Jesus in its historical context. Who is the Son of Man? When will the kingdom come? What is the destiny of Israel? These questions are never directly answered. Apparently, some thought that Jesus would return very soon and make Israel the supreme earthly power. Others thought these were symbolic pictures of the inauguration of a new community of love, living in the power of the Spirit, a community meant to be a beacon of light in the darkness of the world. That is the difference between a magical form of nationalism and a spiritual teaching of universal love.

Third, talk of judgement, eternal life, and punishment, which are central themes of Jesus' teaching, need to be very carefully considered in the light of the teaching that Jesus came to save the lost and give his life as a ransom for many, not simply to condemn the unjust and "unbelievers" to terrible punishment. He preached good news for all, not bad news for most. And he preached that humans, "though they had been judged in the flesh as everyone is judged, they might live in the spirit as God does."[20] For Jesus, judgement is real and inevitable. But his *final* word is that nothing in all creation, and that must clearly include hell itself, can finally resist the love of God.[21]

20. 1 Pet 4:6.

21. Rom 8:39.

SIX

Reconciliation

THE PHARISEE AND THE TAX COLLECTOR: Humility

> He also told this parable to some who trusted in themselves that they were righteous and regarded others with contempt: "Two men went up to the temple to pray, one a Pharisee and the other a tax collector. The Pharisee, standing by himself, was praying thus, 'God, I thank you that I am not like other people: thieves, rogues, adulterers, or even like this tax collector. I fast twice a week; I give a tenth of all my income.' But the tax collector, standing far off, would not even look up to heaven, but was beating his breast and saying, 'God, be merciful to me, a sinner!' I tell you, this man went down to his home justified rather than the other; for all who exalt themselves will be humbled, but all who humble themselves will be exalted."
>
> —Luke 18:9–14

To ENTER THE KINGDOM of heaven it seems that we must be perfectly loving, merciful, and just, for that is the character of those who inherit the kingdom. That is far from easy, and for many it is impossible. "The gate is narrow and the way is hard that leads to life, and there are few who find it."[1] These are stern words, and they have led some Christians to think that only a few will be saved, while the vast majority are on a path that leads to destruction. Ironically, those Christians usually fail to see that, according to the Gospels, the narrow gate is the way of moral perfection, not just the way

1. Matt 7:14.

of devout faith. In effect, since they themselves are usually far from morally perfect, and are often the first to confess that they are "miserable sinners," they often condemn themselves while thinking that they are condemning others.

The Parable of the Pharisee and the Tax Collector is very critical of those who think of themselves as people of devout faith. As an example, Jesus imagines a pious Pharisee, who thanks God because he keeps the rules of morality and of religious observance, and is "not like other men." It is unfortunate that the term "Pharisee" is often still used to mean hypocrite. Not all Pharisees were hypocrites; and Jesus' own teachings are closer to those of the Pharisees than they are to most other Jewish sects of his day. What is meant by "Pharisee" in this parable is a well-respected, pious believer, who in this instance turns out to be proud and self-satisfied in his obedience to the rules of his religion, and who despises others. This parable's teaching is not restricted to one Jewish sect but is applicable to the seemingly pious in any faith, whether Jewish, Muslim, Christian, or any other. In the same way, not all tax collectors take bribes, but the one in this parable is presumed to be doing so. The parable teaches that even those who break moral rules can be justified before God if they are truly penitent, more so than pious believers who are proud and self-righteous. Good works are demanded of us; but in the end what matters is an acknowledgement of our weakness and total dependence upon God.

This is the virtue of humility, but it is easily misunderstood. Humility is not a virtue that occurs in Aristotle's classic list of moral virtues, and Aristotle finds a proper place in his list for pride in one's achievements and even for magnanimous displays of wealth. Aristotle did believe there was a God, but did not think that God created the universe or was concerned with it at all. Jesus, however, believing in a creator God, saw that humility before God was of great importance. It is the recognition that we do not make ourselves, and can claim no merit for our talents and gifts. All we are and have are gifts of God, and humility is the acknowledgement of that fact. There is a place for self-respect and there is no place for grovelling subordination to other people. But before God there should only be gratitude for the gift of life and reverent awe before the One who is the source of all power, wisdom, and love.

Human moral weakness has led some Christians, most notably St. Augustine, to speak of "original sin" or even of "original guilt"—guilt we are born with, even before we have done anything. There is no hint of that idea in Jewish tradition, or in the teachings of the Eastern Orthodox churches. It is mainly found in the Latin and Western traditions of Christianity. The idea of being held guilty before one has done anything, and the idea that we all deserve to be punished for something that someone else (Adam) did, are both morally repugnant. But it does make sense to think that we are brought up in a society that encourages greed and self-seeking—often disguised as reasonable need and self-preservation—and in which belief in a superior spiritual power has faded. This means that it is easier to be selfish than to be altruistic, easier to hate than to love, and easier to believe gossip than to seek the truth. We are all in a "far country," far from the knowledge and love of God, and those who admit this are more prepared to rely on the Spirit of God than those who are content with the habits and prejudices of their own society as sufficient moral guides.

The good are acceptable to God. But true goodness seems to lie beyond human reach. That is why faith—as the giving up of self to allow the Spirit to live and work in one's life—becomes a necessary way to the kingdom. Christian faith is not accepting truths on authority, even though faith presupposes that there is a God. Christian faith is not even just trust in God, though it presupposes that one does trust God's promises. Christian faith is accepting God's Spirit to rule inwardly in one's life. It is this faith that does not claim goodness as its own achievement, but instead cooperates with the divine Spirit to reach a perfection that is given, not earned. This is the secret of the parables of reconciliation.

THE UNFORGIVING SERVANT: Atonement

> For this reason the kingdom of heaven may be compared to a king who wished to settle accounts with his slaves. When he began the reckoning, one who owed him ten thousand talents was brought to him; and, as he could not pay, his lord ordered him to be sold, together with his wife and children and all his possessions, and payment to be made. So the slave fell on his knees before him, saying, "Have patience with me, and I will pay you everything." And out of pity for him, the lord of that slave released him and forgave him the debt. But that same slave, as he went out, came upon one of his fellow slaves who owed him a hundred denarii; and seizing him by the throat, he said, "Pay what you owe." Then his fellow slave fell down and pleaded with him, "Have patience with me, and I will pay you." But he refused; then he went and threw him

> into prison until he would pay the debt. When his fellow slaves saw what had happened, they were greatly distressed, and they went and reported to their lord all that had taken place. Then his lord summoned him and said to him, "You wicked slave! I forgave you all that debt because you pleaded with me. Should you not have had mercy on your fellow slave, as I had mercy on you?" And in anger his lord handed him over to be tortured until he would pay his entire debt. So my heavenly Father will also do to every one of you, if you do not forgive your brother or sister from your heart.
>
> —Matthew 18:23–35

The Parable of the Unforgiving Servant[2] at first sight seems to suggest that in the kingdom of heaven God will treat us as we have treated other people during our life on earth. This seems rather harsh, given the way most of us typically treat others. As so often in Matthew's Gospel, it looks as if the emphasis is on "works," on how we feel and act towards others, not on how much faith we have. And that is going to be very tough for most of us.

In the parable, a king forgives his servant an improbably huge debt, after the servant pleaded for mercy, and promised he would try to pay later. So, it is implied, God will forgive us for wrongdoing if we ask for mercy, and resolve to make some compensation as and how we can. Part of this compensation is to treat others mercifully. When, in the parable, the servant refuses to remit the much smaller debt of a fellow servant, the king sends the unmerciful servant to prison "till he should pay all his debt."

Some readers, including Jeremias, have thought that the servant can never pay such an enormous debt, and so he will be there for ever.[3] But no prison sentence literally lasts for ever. Sentences are for a finite time, and even the longest sentences are ended by death. A reading more compatible with the belief that God is merciful is that the debt may be paid by someone else, if the servant in prison comes to sincerely repent and ask again for mercy. After all, Jesus, the one who tells the parable, is, Christians believe, the one who gives his life to free all from their sins, who "pays the price" of sin,[4] presumably including the sins of those who may be in prison.

It is not that there is a stipulated and unchangeable punishment for sin, and Jesus somehow takes it on himself. That is much too mechanical a view of the atonement, the reconciliation, of humanity and divinity. Rather,

2. Matt 18:23–35.

3. Jeremias, *Rediscovering the Parables*, 166.

4. Eph 1:7.

God in Christ partakes in the suffering of humanity, uniting the life of Jesus to the divine and thus sharing in the fullest sense in the ambiguities and sufferings of human life. Humanity is, in Jesus, united to the divine life, and it is through sharing in that union that we are reconciled to God.

Christ died for our sins, and Jesus gave his life to free us from the slavery of sin. But we are not reconciled to God solely by the death of Jesus; we are reconciled by the risen life of Jesus. It is a life that has experienced and passed through suffering and death, and that is of fundamental importance. But the victory lies in the resurrection life, in which we are invited to share. This is what pays the price of human sin, to accomplish our release from the prison of pride, hatred, and greed, a price no mere human could pay, but which Christ pays in becoming embodied, in suffering and in defeating hatred, in this broken world.

In the parable, the servant's punishment is to lose all that he had, including his wife and children and his own freedom. But the master remits that punishment when the servant asks for mercy and promises to try to repay the debt. The story of an all-powerful king who punishes or forgives at will masks the spiritual teaching that a life of pitiless and unmerciful treatment of others will lead to personal distress and suffering, as we experience for ourselves the sorts of harms we have inflicted on others.

We do not literally owe God money, a debt that God can simply write off if God wishes. But we have taken the gifts of God and used them for selfish personal gain. The purposes of God have been frustrated, and God's gifts misused. We have become what we ought not to be; we have missed the mark of authentic human existence (that is what *hamartia*, a common New Testament word for sin, really means); we have disfigured God's creation; we have imprisoned ourselves in our own greed and vindictiveness.

God can release us from this fate, because God, and only God, can inwardly change our character to one that is able to receive and mediate love. If people are truly free and self-shaping, God cannot do such a thing by the exercise of brute power alone. God has to interact with human souls, to understand us from within our hearts and minds, to persuade us to love, to be self-sacrificial for the sake of others, to care for universal justice and friendship despite mockery and opposition.

The final goal of such loving concern is to establish a loving personal relationship between the Creator and created persons. If forgiveness is to be complete, it must unite the forgiver and the forgiving in friendship. For humans, to do this on earth is often impossible. Those who remain fixed in evil will not desire and will not be able to have true friendship. They isolate themselves by their hatred of others, and they must through hard experience learn the destructive nature of their lives and the possibility of finding fulfilment by sharing with others.

With God all things are possible,[5] and if there is a life in the world to come it will be one in which those who choose the way of destruction and hatred will come to a full realization of the despair to which such a way leads. On that way, God will be present, to offer divine help in turning to the better way that leads to full union with the divine. For God to be forgiving is for God to be prepared to forgive, to unite to the divine life even lives that have been broken, to work positively to prepare hearts to be forgiven, and to work within the inner lives of human persons to reconcile them in a union of mutual love to the source and full actualization of all goodness.

Nevertheless, the parable suggests that forgiveness is only possible if people are themselves forgiving. Without some attempt at reform, the work of forgiveness, even divine forgiveness, cannot begin. God offers forgiveness to all. But that offer must be met by the acceptance of God's love, and by some attempt to change. The unmerciful servant, if he shows no remorse, will be punished (Matthew in typical fashion says "tormented," but we might say, tormented by his own hatred and greed) until his debt is paid.

Bernard Scott sees this parable as very problematic,[6] as the (gentile) king is first unreasonably drastic in assigning such a severe punishment, then very arbitrary in simply retracting his decision, and finally, influenced by the reports of other servants, he goes back on his promise of forgiveness. Thus, in Scott's view, the king is a very ambiguous person morally, and the parable is not at all an allegory of God's treatment of sinners. Instead, he says, it is meant to throw the hearers into moral confusion, and perhaps lead them to conclude that all people alike are in sin, and that mercy does not take account of retributive justice.

Scott's interpretation certainly holds that the parable has a hidden meaning; indeed, so hidden that Matthew completely failed to see it. But the meaning Scott sees seems to subvert any notion that a just and loving life is a condition of entrance into God's kingdom, which is repeatedly stressed in many parables. It is more consistent with the general tenor of the parables, especially of those I considered in the section on "The Moral Demand," to hold that only those whose righteousness exceeds that of the

5. Matt 19:26.

6. Scott, *Hear Then the Parable*, ch. 12.

scribes and Pharisees can enter the kingdom.[7] The problem that leaves is of what happens to those who are not so righteous. The "hidden meaning" of the parable that I am proposing is that God is not literally an all-powerful judge who dispenses rewards and punishments as he sees fit (Scott is right about that). The fictional story is about the inner spiritual life of human beings. It suggests that a life of vindictive treatment of others leads to destruction of the true self, and that liberation from such a life can be found by total and life-changing dependence on the mercy of God. Without openness to such a change, forgiveness remains a possibility, but not yet an actuality.

Perhaps that is the meaning of the mysterious saying, troubling to some, that "People will be forgiven every sin and blasphemy, but blasphemy against the Spirit will not be forgiven . . . either in this age or in the age to come."[8] To say this sin will not be forgiven is to say that there is a form of punishment for it that is inevitable. Yet there is no reason to think that the punishment will be without end. "Blasphemy against the Spirit" is speaking evil of the work of the Spirit, and thus it is a complete refusal of the Spirit of divine love. However, even such a heart can change. Matthew is perhaps at this point rather misleadingly harsh, for Jesus clearly taught that there can be no limit to forgiveness.[9] If that is true of humans, it must also be true of God, who is not less good than humans. Nevertheless, some things need to be punished, because forgiveness has a condition, that persons must will to know and do the good, though they may be ignorant and weak, before the forgiving and reconciling power of the Spirit can work in them.

Accepting the power of the Spirit is faith. Faith is not effective without some personal effort to turn to the good, which entails trying to be merciful. Faith is the acceptance that one cannot do this in one's own strength, so that one needs to receive the life of the Spirit of Christ, the Spirit of suffering and triumphant love, into one's own life. Faith is not just having a specific intellectual belief (even an intellectual belief that Jesus is Lord, for example). Faith is actually *living in the power of the Spirit*, and in that way real faith already includes transformation of life, and it is in such transformation that divine forgiveness consists. Faith is not, when fully understood, to be contrasted with "works," as Matthew stresses, for it is faith, understood as the reception of the Spirit, that enables us to act as God demands, that enables us to share in the divine life, and that effects our reconciliation with God.

7. Matt 5:20.

8. Matt 12:31–32.

9. Matt 18:22.

Divine forgiveness, then, is not overlooking evil. It is God's positive action to change human hearts and unite them to the divine life. In the kingdom, God will not after all treat us just as we have treated others. If that were true, very few would survive. But God commands us to treat others mercifully, and it is only when we try, even if we often fail, that he will create in us new hearts that are capable of being united to the divine nature. To be so united to God, one must receive the Spirit of God, who will bring about in us what we are unable to achieve by ourselves.

THE LOST SHEEP AND THE LOST COIN: The return

> Take care that you do not despise one of these little ones; for, I tell you, in heaven their angels continually see the face of my Father in heaven. What do you think? If a shepherd has a hundred sheep, and one of them has gone astray, does he not leave the ninety-nine on the mountains and go in search of the one that went astray? And if he finds it, truly I tell you, he rejoices over it more than over the ninety-nine that never went astray. So it is not the will of your Father in heaven that one of these little ones should be lost.
>
> —Matthew 18:10–14

> Now all the tax collectors and sinners were coming near to listen to him. And the Pharisees and the scribes were grumbling and saying, "This fellow welcomes sinners and eats with them."
>
> So he told them this parable: "Which one of you, having a hundred sheep and losing one of them, does not leave the ninety-nine in the wilderness and go after the one that is lost until he finds it? When he has found it, he lays it on his shoulders and rejoices. And when he comes home, he calls together his friends and neighbors, saying to them, 'Rejoice with me, for I have found my sheep that was lost.' Just so, I tell you, there will be more joy in heaven over one sinner who repents than over ninety-nine righteous persons who need no repentance.
>
> Or what woman having ten silver coins, if she loses one of them, does not light a lamp, sweep the house, and search carefully until she finds it? When she has found it, she calls together her friends and neighbors, saying, 'Rejoice with me, for I have found the coin that I had lost.' Just so, I tell you, there is joy in the presence of the angels of God over one sinner who repents."
>
> —Luke 15:1–10

The kingdom of God will be a world in which all are wholly dependent upon God, all are just and righteous, and all are merciful. This may make the kingdom unattainable for ordinary humans, and even less attainable for those who are less than conventionally good. Yet Jesus shocked his hearers by insisting that God cared for those who are not humble, just, or merciful.

The two Parables of the Lost Sheep and the Lost Coin—the first in Matthew and Luke, the second only in Luke—make the point very sharply by saying that "there will be more joy in heaven over one sinner who repents than over ninety-nine righteous people who need no repentance."[10] I do not suppose it is being suggested that there are people who really need no repentance. Rather, as Jeremias suggests, there are people (they would include most Pharisees) who have not committed major crimes. But, of course, there is much of which they should repent, though they often seem not to realize that.

Furthermore, it is not true that God values repentant sinners more than the piously just. It is only that joy follows repentance, a joy in which the truly righteous will share, as created beings are brought back into union with God. Penitence for sin is not a matter of weeping and self-hatred. It is a matter of great joy, a joy in which all will share. There is exaggeration here, which is typical of Jesus' teaching, making his sayings more memorable, less capable of very literalistic interpretations, but expressive of surprising spiritual truths.

Dominic Crossan points out that Luke uses the parable to defend Jesus' practice of welcoming sinners against the judgmental attitudes of some Pharisees.[11] Matthew puts it rather differently, making the parable counsel against placing stumbling blocks in the path of members of the church community. "It is not the will of your Father in heaven that one of these little ones should be lost," he writes. The parable is thus given slightly different morals in the two Gospels, but the underlying sentiment is the same, that God cares even, or especially, for those who have lost their way in life. This is an example of the way in which parables are typically polyvalent. They do not just have one "correct" meaning, but can be used in different contexts as applications of an underlying principle that is clear in its general orientation, but not rigidly defined.

10. Luke 15:7.

11. Crossan, *The Power of Parable*, ch. 2.

Jesus said of himself, "I was sent only to the *lost sheep* of the house of Israel."[12] It is a constant theme of his teaching that those who enter the kingdom will be the poor and the penitent, while many devout people of faith (as we have seen, rather misleadingly called "the scribes and Pharisees") may find themselves excluded. To put this in contemporary terms, it is the sex workers and money launderers who, if they turn to God, will enter the kingdom. The constant church-goers who proclaim their faith and obedience by saying the Creed every week, may, to their astonishment, find themselves excluded.

But this seems to swing from one impossibly difficult teaching to another. First Jesus seems to say that only the morally perfect will enter the kingdom. But in the next parable he says that the morally perfect will be excluded, and that it is only those who sin long and hard, and then repent at the last moment, who will be welcomed into the kingdom.

This cannot be right. Jesus' teaching is mysterious, but it is not self-contradictory. We need to say that the kingdom of God, when it comes in its fullness, will be a kingdom of perfect mercy, justice, and love. There will be no place there for anger, hatred, resentment, or pride. Those who strive for perfect righteousness are few, and those who succeed are fewer. Here talk of a narrow gate is quite in order. Sadly, moral hypocrisy and deceitfulness are common, even among supposedly upright citizens—in the Parable of the Prodigal Son, the elder son who was obedient to his father, but was actually filled with anger and envy, is a clear case in point. And it could be that even those who seem to succeed are aware of ways in which they fail. For most of us, the path of self-won perfection seems impossible.

So it is that a confession of sin and a plea for forgiveness is appropriate for the vast majority of people, and probably for all. Jesus does not recommend sinning so that repentance can be really worthwhile. But Jesus does assure us that no person is beyond the possibility of repentance and forgiveness. It is when we cease to rely on our own strength of will, and turn to God for forgiveness and help, that the Spirit may "come near" and shape us towards the greater perfection of love that the final kingdom requires.

THE PRODIGAL SON: The door of repentance is always open

> There was a man who had two sons. The younger of them said to his father, "Father, give me the share of the property that will

12. Matt 15:24.

> belong to me." So he divided his property between them. A few days later the younger son gathered all he had and traveled to a distant country, and there he squandered his property in dissolute living. When he had spent everything, a severe famine took place throughout that country, and he began to be in need. So he went and hired himself out to one of the citizens of that country, who sent him to his fields to feed the pigs. He would gladly have filled himself with the pods that the pigs were eating; and no one gave him anything. But when he came to himself he said, "How many of my father's hired hands have bread enough and to spare, but here I am dying of hunger! I will get up and go to my father, and I will say to him, 'Father, I have sinned against heaven and before you; I am no longer worthy to be called your son; treat me like one of your hired hands.'" So he set off and went to his father. But while he was still far off, his father saw him and was filled with compassion; he ran and put his arms around him and kissed him. Then the son said to him, "Father, I have sinned against heaven and before you; I am no longer worthy to be called your son." But the father said to his slaves, "Quickly, bring out a robe—the best one—and put it on him; put a ring on his finger and sandals on his feet. And get the fatted calf and kill it, and let us eat and celebrate; for this son of mine was dead and is alive again; he was lost and is found!" And they began to celebrate.
>
> Now his elder son was in the field; and when he came and approached the house, he heard music and dancing. He called one of the slaves and asked what was going on. He replied, "Your brother has come, and your father has killed the fatted calf, because he has got him back safe and sound." Then he became angry and refused to go in. His father came out and began to plead with him. But he answered his father, "Listen! For all these years I have been working like a slave for you, and I have never disobeyed your command; yet you have never given me even a young goat so that I might celebrate with my friends. But when this son of yours came back, who has devoured your property with prostitutes, you killed the fatted calf for him!" Then the father said to him, "Son, you are always with me, and all that is mine is yours. But we had to celebrate and rejoice, because this brother of yours was dead and has come to life; he was lost and has been found."
>
> —Luke 15:11–32

Luke's Parable of the Prodigal Son expands on that thought. A son who goes to a far country and squanders his inheritance on luxurious living ends up in dire poverty, and returns home in shame, asking to be accepted only as a servant. His father, however, runs out to meet and embrace him, and organizes a great feast to celebrate his return. His brother, who had remained at home and obeyed his father, was angry and refused to attend the feast. We are not told what happened next, except that his father said that it was fitting to rejoice, because the prodigal son "was dead and has come to life; he was lost and has been found."

This is a crucial parable that shows that the dead can return to life, that those who have been on the way to destruction can be received with joy if only they come to their senses and return home.

Dodd and Jeremias agree that this parable was originally Jesus' vindication of his preaching to and eating with the poor and outcast, and was a criticism of the religious purists' objections to this conduct (symbolized by the attitude of the elder son), and perhaps a plea to them to rejoice with the restoration of the penitent.[13]

Dominic Crossan sees the parable as a contrast-parable, which shocks by apparently approving of a wastrel son and disapproving of a dutiful son, and so challenges or even undermines conventional ideas of good and bad.[14]

Bernard Scott also stresses that the elder son, who is jealous and angry, was nevertheless not rejected, for the father assures the elder that everything the father possesses will be his. This, Scott holds, subverts the idea that the younger son (sinners or Christians) is accepted while the elder (the Pharisees or Israel) is rejected. For both are accepted; what the parable does is to commend universal human solidarity, and undercut any attempt to divide the world into insiders and outsiders, good and bad. It is all grace, and the kingdom subverts both moral and legal expectations.[15]

There is, however, no reason why the posited challenge to conventional ideas of good and bad, or the "original situation" of vindicating Jesus' association with the unclean should be the only or even the main points of the parable. The parable easily and properly generalizes into a statement about God's care for sinners and criticism of those who consider themselves religiously or morally pure and superior, and who resent association with the "unrighteous." There are generalized moral principles present, and these principles only work when allegories are employed—when the father

13. Dodd, *The Parables of the Kingdom*, 89–90; Jeremias, *Rediscovering the Parables*, 101ff.

14. Crossan, *The Power of Parable*, ch. 3.

15. Scott, *Hear Then the Parable*, ch. 2.

is assumed to represent God (only in some respects, obviously), and when the elder son is taken to represent pious believers, for example. There is also a clear christological implication that the father's conduct illustrates Jesus' attitude to sinners, so that Jesus' actions show what God is like. Moral, christological, and allegorical aspects of the parable really were implicit in the assumed original versions. Even if they were developed by the Gospel editors in various ways, that development was entirely natural. It remains true for all people everywhere that while the way of moral perfection is almost impossibly difficult (and possibly most difficult for those who think themselves most pure), placing oneself in total dependence on the mercy of God will be met by the surprising recognition that God runs to embrace us as we seek to return.

THE WORKERS IN THE VINEYARD: The gift of eternal life

> For the kingdom of heaven is like a landowner who went out early in the morning to hire laborers for his vineyard. After agreeing with the laborers for the usual daily wage, he sent them into his vineyard. When he went out about nine o'clock, he saw others standing idle in the marketplace; and he said to them, "You also go into the vineyard, and I will pay you whatever is right." So they went. When he went out again about noon and about three o'clock, he did the same. And about five o'clock he went out and found others standing around; and he said to them, "Why are you standing here idle all day?" They said to him, "Because no one has hired us." He said to them, "You also go into the vineyard." When evening came, the owner of the vineyard said to his manager, "Call the laborers and give them their pay, beginning with the last and then going to the first." When those hired about five o'clock came, each of them received the usual daily wage. Now when the first came, they thought they would receive more; but each of them also received the usual daily wage. And when they received it, they grumbled against the landowner, saying, "These last worked only one hour, and you have made them equal to us who have borne the burden of the day and the scorching heat." But he replied to one of them, "Friend, I am doing you no wrong; did you not agree with me for the usual daily wage? Take what belongs to you and go; I choose to give to this last the same as I give to you. Am I not allowed to do what I choose with what belongs to me? Or are you

envious because I am generous?" So the last will be first, and the first will be last.

—Matthew 20:1–16

Jesus' teaching is that God comes to meet us as we seek to return to God. But one parable, at least, goes even further than that. It is a parable that suggests that God will give to all who return to God much more than they could possibly desire or deserve.

Matthew tells of a rich man who asked Jesus what he had to do to inherit eternal life. Jesus told him to give away all his possessions. The rich man turned away, but Peter then complained that he and his companions had given up everything to follow Jesus, and asked, "What then will we have?" Jesus, in reply, tells a parable about a landowner who employed workers at various hours of the day, from 9 in the morning until 5 at night. At the end of the day, the landowner paid them all the same wage, and the ones who had worked all day complained that they deserved more than the others.

The point seems to be that God gives eternal life to all who seek it. In particular, God gives eternal life to penitent sinners and outcasts, as well as to Pharisees who have kept the divine Law all their lives. This may seem unjust, though the owner had agreed what those who worked longest would be paid, so the situation is that those who had only worked for a short while were paid the same. There is no dishonesty involved.

There is a rather similar Mahayana Buddhist story (the Parable of the Burning House) in the Lotus Sutra, that people would work for various degrees of liberation, and expect to be rewarded with chariots of various sizes, small, medium, or large. But in the event, all were given magnificent and large chariots. This is a sign, not of injustice, but, in the Buddhist case, of the immense compassion of the Buddha. In the Christian case, workers should not complain that they deserve more than people who seem to have given up less, for God's gift of eternal life is free. As Jesus says, "Many who are first will be last, and the last will be first."[16] Those who have pride of place in religious piety may end up with the same reward as those who even at the last moment cry for mercy and forgiveness. As with the Parable of the Prodigal Son, envy and jealousy are unacceptable in the kingdom, and the better response is one of joy at the good fortune of the "last."

16. Matt 19:30.

The good news that Jesus preaches is that no one, however debased, is ever beyond the reach of God's redeeming and transforming love. "Neither death, nor life, nor angels, nor rulers, nor things present, nor things to come . . . nor anything else in all creation, will be able to separate us from the love of God in Christ Jesus."[17] It follows that if anyone says that death can separate us from God's love, that after death they will have no further hope of union with God, they have not seen the range and power of divine love. Even in the world to come, God will continue to seek those who are lost in hatred, greed, and pride, and call them home.

Jesus' mission was to turn the hearts and minds of those walking towards destruction towards the God who, like the father of the prodigal son, was longing to meet and embrace them. The perfection of the kingdom is the gift of the Spirit. The entrance to it is by reliance not on one's own merits, but on God, who welcomes all to share in eternal joy. That is the "good news," the gospel, of the rule of God, who has come near in and through the person of Jesus.

17. Rom 8:31–39.

SEVEN

The Supreme Good

THE PEARL AND THE BURIED TREASURE: Sharing in the divine goodness

> The kingdom of heaven is like treasure hidden in a field, which someone found and hid; then in his joy he goes and sells all that he has and buys that field.
>
> Again, the kingdom of heaven is like a merchant in search of fine pearls; on finding one pearl of great value, he went and sold all that he had and bought it.
>
> —Matthew 13:44–46

THE KINGDOM OF HEAVEN is like a valuable pearl, or like a great treasure, so desirable that it is worth selling all one has to obtain it.

In accordance with his general theme that parables aim to confront people with a decision, and challenge them to apply their answer in their lives, Professor Dodd says that these parables "are not intended to illustrate any general maxim, but to enforce an appeal which Jesus was making for a specific course of action."[1] Jesus was indeed making an appeal that the disciples should be prepared to give up all and seek first the kingdom.[2] But this, despite what Dodd says, entails a general maxim. For there is a reason for giving up all, namely, that there is a supreme good, and that the way to find it is to follow Jesus. This is both the statement of a general maxim

1. Dodd, *The Parables of the Kingdom*, 85.
2. Matt 6:33.

(in fact, two general maxims, the existence of a supreme good, and what the way to it is) and an appeal to make a positive response. We need not distinguish between stating general maxims and making specific appeals, for though they are logically distinct both these things go together. Without the general maxim, the appeal would be arbitrary and even irrational. With it, it makes perfect sense.

As Joachim Jeremias says, these short parables are basically about joy.[3] One of the fruits of the Spirit is joy, but that may be joy in the ordinary things of life, in the beauty of hills and mountains, or loving friendship, or the discovery of a new truth.

Accepting the rule of God is not gritting one's teeth and vowing to obey God's laws, however difficult. It is finding a joy that surpasses all others, and that cannot ever be taken away ("Your hearts will rejoice, and no one will take your joy from you").[4] Is there a joy that surpasses all others?

For many people, such an idea would not make much sense. There are many different things that make people happy, and different people find happiness in many different ways. There are also many different things that people value, or think are worthwhile. Some people will think the possession of an original painting is worth millions, while others would not care whether they possessed such a thing or not. Some people will pay a great deal to go to an opera, while others would pay a great deal never to see an opera again. Perhaps, some people think, happiness is all a matter of taste, of doing something one desires, and there is no accounting for taste, or no way of saying that some tastes are better than others.

Suppose, however, that there is a God who has created us for a purpose. This purpose will be to bring about good things that would otherwise not exist. There may indeed be very many different sorts of good things, and what we think is good will largely depend on the sort of tastes and temperaments we have. God is the ultimate source of all good things,[5] and God wills that we should be the means of bringing many of them about, of creating and appreciating them for what they are.

As well as being the source of all goodness, the divine being is itself supremely good. When you say that something is good, you mean that it is worth existing, just for its own sake. If someone was swimming in a beautiful pool, with the sun shining, and lots of friends surrounding her,

3. Jeremias, *Rediscovering the Parables*, 156ff.

4. John 16:22.

5. Jas 1:17.

it would be absurd to ask whether that experience is good. Of course, it is good. It is worth doing just for its own sake.

There are lots of things that are good just for their own sakes—seeing a glorious sunset, discovering the answer to a difficult puzzle, hearing a well-played piece of music, constructing a piece of furniture, these are all good. They are experiences worth having. It is the experience that makes it good. A sunset that nobody sees is neither bad nor good; it just is. It is seeing and enjoying the sunset that is good; it is just a worthwhile experience to have.

You might say, then, that beauty lies in eye of the beholder. If there were no beholders there would be no beauty. Yet it is not true that anything we enjoy is good. The enjoyment is good, but you have to ask whether what you enjoy is really worth enjoying. If somebody enjoyed torturing babies, that would not be good. So you have to think about the object, the thing you think is good, as well as the subjective experience of pleasure and satisfaction.

If there was such a thing as supreme goodness, it would lie in the pleasurable experience of something that was the most worthwhile thing possible. Goodness is a combination of personal experience and an object or process that is really worthwhile. God is a being of the greatest possible wisdom, creative power, and love, who knows all the worthwhile things that can ever exist in the most intense way possible. That is what it means to say that God is supremely good. God has beatitude, perfect bliss, in knowing and contemplating that which is supremely worthwhile; and that is the being of God itself.

Yet this may seem like a rather solitary or even selfish sort of goodness. A God who is supremely happy in contemplating the divine perfection is not really a God of love, who delights in making other beings happy and who shares the divine happiness and perfection with others.

The Christian perception of God is precisely that "God is love (*agape*)."[6] A God of supreme goodness will be a God who shares the divine wisdom, happiness, and creativity with others. God will create other personal beings, who will have their own creativity, who will be able to know and love all the beauties of the created world, and who can cooperate with others in bringing about new activities and experiences that will be shared with others.

When we say that people are good, we often mean that they act to enrich the personal lives of other individuals and wider communities. They

6. 1 John 4:8.

are people who desire that others, and if possible all sentient beings, should share in the sort of happiness and fulfilment that they desire, or in whatever is the equivalent for them. Such action expands the ability of personal lives to take pleasure in contemplating and in creating new enriching states. We call persons good when they cooperate to help others to live rich and fruitful lives. In doing so, they also enrich their own lives by helping to create new forms of goodness that they could not bring about on their own. True goodness lies in a combination of happiness in personal excellence and cooperation with others so that all may share in that happiness.

This gives us a good idea of what the final and fulfilled kingdom of God is. It is a society of persons who cooperate in creating new possibilities of being and happiness. It is not a static state where nothing new ever happens. It is a dynamic and creative world of interrelated persons, who rejoice in the world that flows from the uncreated and supremely perfect and personal Source of all beings.

This world does not exist by chance or by good luck. It exists because there is a supremely perfect God who creates a world that is beautiful and intelligible, and creates persons who can cooperate in creating and appreciating new forms of beauty, intelligibility, and friendship. It is a world not ruled by fate, but by an orientation to goodness. The God on whom this world depends, without whom it would not exist, contains in the divine being itself complete knowledge and the fullest appreciation of all the goods that exist, and cooperates with created persons to create endlessly new forms of goodness. If we could know God fully, we would have a share in that total knowledge and love of goodness, and we would cooperate with God's purpose to realize ever new forms of goodness in the world. In such a world, God would rule, not by force but by the attraction of the perfect.

When Crossan briefly discusses these parables,[7] he sees them as calling for a reversal of all previous values and openness to "a new world and unforeseen possibilities." I have no problem with this interpretation, but I think that there is not just a present openness to new possibilities, but also a real future for humanity and for the whole created universe, when evil has been decisively ended, and all things rest in the love and knowledge of God.

The kingdom of God is the ultimate goal of creation, the fulfilment of all rightly ordered desires. It is the pearl of priceless worth, an eternal treasure hidden in the fields of time.

7. Crossan, *In Parables*, 14.

THE KINGDOM OF GOD

Jesus was apparently often asked when the kingdom would be fully realized. It seems that many human prayers for justice, throughout the whole of human history, are not answered, except in the sense that evil brings destruction on itself, only to be succeeded by new forms of evil. There has been no successful history of a lasting Utopia in the history of humanity, and the establishment of the Christian church was certainly no such thing.

As long as the freedom and temptation to do evil remains, the kingdom of God will not come in its fullness. Yet that is not to say that it has not already come in a more inward way, in the hearts of men and women. That is why believers form "an elect," a body of people chosen to witness to kingdom values in a fallen world. They are an imperfect elect, but nevertheless their union with God makes a real difference to how they feel, think, and act. Like the Jews and their original and still binding covenant, the Christian churches are a very mixed bunch, but they are meant to be like yeast in dough or like light in darkness.

How long will this realm of freedom remain? We have no idea. In the early church, and indeed throughout the church's history, there have been many who have looked for a cataclysmic divine intervention into history, a literal sudden and unexpected return of Christ to earth in glory. Their hopes have always been disappointed, and I think such an event would sadly cut off the possibility of many good and creative developments in the future story of humanity.

It is true, nevertheless, that, like many Old Testament prophets, Jesus looked not only for an ambiguous coming of the kingdom in human hearts, but for a final coming of the kingdom in a fully God-centred community from which evil and suffering had been excluded. In the case of the prophets, predictions of a glorious political triumph of Israel over the other nations of the world was never fulfilled in any literal way. The triumph of goodness for which they looked was never in fact quite so nationalistic. It lies, like the resurrection life of Jesus, in a realm beyond this historical time and space.

It is the kingdom of heaven, where Abraham and the patriarchs, Mary and the saints, already live in the open presence of God. That kingdom is one that God wills every human soul to enter, when this world—this whole cosmos—has passed away. What we now experience of the rule of God is a series of fractured images of eternity appearing in our spacetime, like shafts of light breaking through storm clouds. This spiritual realm is real, not just a subjective mental feeling, but it is not in our time or space. It gives us a hope for a future in which we can exist, but it is not either a hope for some future political state in the ordinary historical process or for a sudden ending of life on this planet by an unexpected and miraculous divine act.

It seems that Jesus certainly held out hope for a full realization of the kingdom, and the New Testament records that some disciples thought it referred to the restoration of Israel as a socio-political state. It seems certain that, as a man, he had no idea of the vastness of our physical cosmos, and it is honestly recorded that he simply did not know when the kingdom would come in its fullness.[8]

When he said that the kingdom had "come near," one natural interpretation of this is that the rule of God in "heaven," the spiritual realm, was in him breaking through into the historical world in a new way. If it is true that he spoke of himself as "Son of Man" and as the Davidic King, it seems that he thought of himself as the leader or mediator of a new covenant, or bond of unity, between God and a new community of the Spirit. If after his physical death he appeared in some form in the historical world, then it could properly be said that the Son of Man had appeared with spiritual power and in the glory of the Father.

There is an unusual but highly appropriate word for this. It is the word "prolepsis." It means the representation of a future state as if it was present. The appearance of Jesus to the disciples after his physical death was a prolepsis of the ultimate kingdom, a representation of a future state, the lives of humans united in love with God, as already existing. It is as though we could say, "I see the future; it is here!" We would not want to say, "The future goal is a very long way ahead; it may take aeons to appear." And we would not want to say, "The future goal will instantaneously be reached tomorrow or the day after." We might rather say, "The future goal is certain; it is rooted in eternity; for some (Jesus, and the dead who are in the presence of God) it already exists; I have felt something of that eternity; it draws me to itself at this very moment."

So the answer to the question, "when will the goal be reached?" is, "It is not for you to know that; what is important is that it will be reached, that it already exists on a spiritual plane; that you can reach it, and that what you do now will shape your entrance into it."

8. Matt 24:36: "But about that day and hour no one knows, neither the angels of heaven, nor the Son."

THE ORIGIN AND GOAL OF CREATION

It might be helpful to compare the biblical story of creation in Genesis with the images for the end or fulfilment of all creation that developed in the Jewish faith and were adopted by Jesus. It is generally accepted that the Genesis creation story is not literally true. As St. Augustine said, creation does not actually take God six days. Creation is the dependence of all things at all times on God, and it applies to each present moment, not just to the beginning of the universe.[9] To say that the universe is created is to say that each moment flows from and is wholly dependent upon God, a supremely perfect reality beyond our space and time. The Genesis story has important points to make about the ultimate goodness of creation, about the supremacy of God, and about the responsibility of humans. But it is not a literal account that competes with modern scientific knowledge.

In a similar way, images for the goal and end of creation do not compete with scientific accounts of how the physical universe will end. They say that good will ultimately triumph over evil, that God is a God of universal love whose purpose will be realized, and that humans will be able consciously to share in that final purpose. This will not happen next year, and it will not happen anywhere in a universe where the laws of decay are as they are in this universe. As creation did not take a week, but billions of years, and is still in process, so the fulfilment of all things will not be next week, but is being built up at every moment as each moment enters into God and is there transformed into the life of eternity. As in creation each moment flows *from* God, so in the fulfilment of all things each moment returns *to* God and becomes, in a transfigured form, part of the divine being.[10]

Prayer that the kingdom of God will come, on earth as in heaven, is therefore perhaps best thought of as a prayer for a foreshadowing, a prolepsis, of the ultimate goal of being in present lives. William Blake wrote that, even now in this present moment, you might "hold infinity in the palm of your hand, and eternity in an hour."[11] The rule of God has come near, and we can know and feel it begin to grow within us. Jesus will not literally come again to this earth, descending from the clouds with hosts of angels and the resurrected dead. But the glorified Jesus will be fully

9. Augustine, *On the Literal Meaning of Genesis*.

10. This view is explored at greater length in my *Sharing in the Divine Nature*.

11. William Blake, "Auguries of Innocence." https://www.poetryfoundation.org/poems/43650/auguries-of-innocence.

revealed when a renewed cosmos is created, when all those who have died in history will be seen in their renewed lives, and when all the good things of this world are fulfilled in a new world that will never decay or die. Christ will appear again in glory, and we shall see him, as we shall see all things united and fulfilled in God.

As the Synoptic Gospels show, Jesus taught these things in parables. Those parables have a hidden meaning, a secret that is hidden in plain sight. The secret is this: with Jesus, the rule of God has been manifested in time in a definitive way. There are many who are touched and changed by the eternal without recognizing it as other than a moral demand of love and compassion. But the rule of God on earth has been uniquely expressed in the person of Jesus, and continues, if only ambiguously and partially, in the inward community of the Spirit of suffering and indestructible love that he embodied. In this paradigmatic form, the eternal enters into time, in order that time may be assumed into eternity.

Bibliography

Borg, Marcus. *Meeting Jesus Again for the First Time: The Historical Jesus and the Heart of Contemporary Faith.* San Francisco: Harper Collins, 1994.

Crossan, Dominic. *In Parables: The Challenge of the Historical Jesus.* San Francisco: Harper & Row, 1985.

———. *The Power of Parable: How Fiction by Jesus Became Fiction about Jesus.* San Francisco: Harper Collins, 2012.

Dante Alighieri. *The Inferno.* Translated by Henry Cary. New York: Collier, 1885.

Dodd, C. H. *The Parables of the Kingdom.* 1935. Reprint, London: Fontana, 1961.

Funk, Robert. *Jesus as Precursor.* Minneapolis: Fortress, 1975.

Harnack, Adolf. *What Is Christianity?* Translated by T. B. Saunders. San Diego: Book Tree, 2006.

Jeremias, Joachim. *Rediscovering the Parables.* Translated by S. H. Hooke. London: SCM, 1963.

Jülicher, Adoph. *Die Gleichnisreden Jesu.* Freiburg: Mohr (Siebeck), 1899.

Lessing, Gottfried. "On the Proof of the Spirit and of Power" (1777). Translated by Henry Chadwick in *Lessing's Theological Writings: Selections in Translation.* London: A & C Black, 1956.

Neusner, Jacob. "Is the God of Judaism Incarnate?" *Religious Studies* 24.2 (1988) 213–38.

Schweitzer, Albert. *The Quest of the Historical Jesus.* Edited by John Bowden. London: SCM, 2000.

Scott, Bernard. *Hear Then the Parable: A Commentary on the Parables of Jesus.* Minneapolis: Fortress, 1989.

Snodgrass, Klyne R. *Stories with Intent: A Comprehensive Guide to the Parables of Jesus.* 2nd ed. Grand Rapids: Eerdmans, 2018.

Theissen, Gerd, and Annette Merz. *The Historical Jesus: A Comprehensive Guide.* Translated by John Bowden. London: SCM, 1998.

Via, Dan Otto. *The Parables: Their Literary and Existential Dimension.* Minneapolis: Fortress, 1967.

Ward, Keith. *Religion in the Modern World: Celebrating Pluralism and Diversity.* Cambridge: Cambridge University Press, 2019

———. *Sharing the Divine Nature: A Personalist Metaphysics.* Eugene, OR: Cascade, 2020.

Problems:

1. Why the need for a unique union of divine & human
2. What is a 'personal God'? p9.
3. What is 'that cosmic figure of Christ'? p10
4. Why would Jesus believe that he was an embodiment of wisdom
5. How would you know that you had 'a more intense sense of the
6. Did Jesus transform Judaism? p11
7. Can you have a relationship with a God who is Love? p12
8. Aren't unity & relationship different? p13
9. Is creation new or evolving? p15
10. Did Jesus think about Jesus? p16
11. 'A new bond between humanity & divinity' p19
12. 'Near' isn't 'here & now'. p20
13. Was Jesus a human embodiment of divine Wisdom? p21
14. 'A transcendent God' - meaningless? p21
15. Are parables illustrative of moral principles or are they abou
16. Aren't parables more than allegories - they relate directly t
17. Rule of God in Jesus - quite an authorative claim! p23
18. KW believes in a future appearance & present reality - cake &
19. Surely, already present in everyone? p25
20. Not sure about doctrine; isn't it about 'try it & see'? p25
21. Denial of a spiritual goal; isn't now enough - life is for now
22. Why isn't love enough? p25
23. Love has never been about perfection p26
24. Surely the P of Good Samaritan is about prejudice? p26
25. Surely the P of Prod. Son is about love? p26
26. Surely longing for immortality is self-centred? p27
27. Beyond death who knows? p27
28. Surely, Jesus is not about morality - about absolutes of
29. What are 'ordinary moral values'? p27
30. What is 'God's point of view'? p.27
31. God is not an object p28 or true - God could be Existence
34. Surely, the truth is we don't know about life after death
35. Why all this objectivity (idolatry). Truth, beauty & goodness
36. Did Jesus accept the Torah - surely, only the parts that
37. Liberator from sin - again an 'objective' outlook? p29
38. A little unfair to Crossan - he is comparing

Lightning Source UK Ltd.
Milton Keynes UK
UKHW041506160821
388947UK00003B/942

9 781725 288430

39. Be careful with judgements; we are all entitled to make sense
40. Magic stuff - Jesus is God - what an amazing claim! p30